Mome

TEST PREPARATION



# Regents

## Success Strategies Global History and Geography

# DEAR FUTURE EXAM SUCCESS STORY

First of all, **THANK YOU** for purchasing Mometrix study materials!

Second, congratulations! You are one of the few determined test-takers who are committed to doing whatever it takes to excel on your exam. **You have come to the right place.** We developed these study materials with one goal in mind: to deliver you the information you need in a format that's concise and easy to use.

In addition to optimizing your guide for the content of the test, we've outlined our recommended steps for breaking down the preparation process into small, attainable goals so you can make sure you stay on track.

We've also analyzed the entire test-taking process, identifying the most common pitfalls and showing how you can overcome them and be ready for any curveball the test throws you.

Standardized testing is one of the biggest obstacles on your road to success, which only increases the importance of doing well in the high-pressure, high-stakes environment of test day. Your results on this test could have a significant impact on your future, and this guide provides the information and practical advice to help you achieve your full potential on test day.

**Your success is our success**

**We would love to hear from you!** If you would like to share the story of your exam success or if you have any questions or comments in regard to our products, please contact us at **800-673-8175** or **support@mometrix.com**.

Thanks again for your business and we wish you continued success!

Sincerely,
The Mometrix Test Preparation Team


Written and edited by the Mometrix Test Preparation Team
Printed in the United States of America

# TABLE OF CONTENTS

# Introduction

**Thank you for purchasing this resource**! You have made the choice to prepare yourself for a test that could have a huge impact on your future, and this guide is designed to help you be fully ready for test day. Obviously, it's important to have a solid understanding of the test material, but you also need to be prepared for the unique environment and stressors of the test, so that you can perform to the best of your abilities.

For this purpose, the first section that appears in this guide is the **Success Strategies**. We've devoted countless hours to meticulously researching what works and what doesn't, and we've boiled down our findings to the five most impactful steps you can take to improve your performance on the test. We start at the beginning with study planning and move through the preparation process, all the way to the testing strategies that will help you get the most out of what you know when you're finally sitting in front of the test.

We recommend that you start preparing for your test as far in advance as possible. However, if you've bought this guide as a last-minute study resource and only have a few days before your test, we recommend that you skip over the first two Success Strategies since they address a long-term study plan.

If you struggle with **test anxiety**, we strongly encourage you to check out our recommendations for how you can overcome it. Test anxiety is a formidable foe, but it can be beaten, and we want to make sure you have the tools you need to defeat it.

# Strategy #1 – Plan Big, Study Small

There's a lot riding on your performance. If you want to ace this test, you're going to need to keep your skills sharp and the material fresh in your mind. You need a plan that lets you review everything you need to know while still fitting in your schedule. We'll break this strategy down into three categories.

## Information Organization

Start with the information you already have: the official test outline. From this, you can make a complete list of all the concepts you need to cover before the test. Organize these concepts into groups that can be studied together, and create a list of any related vocabulary you need to learn so you can brush up on any difficult terms. You'll want to keep this vocabulary list handy once you actually start studying since you may need to add to it along the way.

## Time Management

Once you have your set of study concepts, decide how to spread them out over the time you have left before the test. Break your study plan into small, clear goals so you have a manageable task for each day and know exactly what you're doing. Then just focus on one small step at a time. When you manage your time this way, you don't need to spend hours at a time studying. Studying a small block of content for a short period each day helps you retain information better and avoid stressing over how much you have left to do. You can relax knowing that you have a plan to cover everything in time. In order for this strategy to be effective though, you have to start studying early and stick to your schedule. Avoid the exhaustion and futility that comes from last-minute cramming!

## Study Environment

The environment you study in has a big impact on your learning. Studying in a coffee shop, while probably more enjoyable, is not likely to be as fruitful as studying in a quiet room. It's important to keep distractions to a minimum. You're only planning to study for a short block of time, so make the most of it. Don't pause to check your phone or get up to find a snack. It's also important to **avoid multitasking**. Research has consistently shown that multitasking will make your studying dramatically less effective. Your study area should also be comfortable and well-lit so you don't have the distraction of straining your eyes or sitting on an uncomfortable chair.

The time of day you study is also important. You want to be rested and alert. Don't wait until just before bedtime. Study when you'll be most likely to comprehend and remember. Even better, if you know what time of day your test will be, set that time aside for study. That way your brain will be used to working on that subject at that specific time and you'll have a better chance of recalling information.

Finally, it can be helpful to team up with others who are studying for the same test. Your actual studying should be done in as isolated an environment as possible, but the work of organizing the information and setting up the study plan can be divided up. In between study sessions, you can discuss with your teammates the concepts that you're all studying and quiz each other on the details. Just be sure that your teammates are as serious about the test as you are. If you find that your study time is being replaced with social time, you might need to find a new team.

# Strategy #2 – Make Your Studying Count

You're devoting a lot of time and effort to preparing for this test, so you want to be absolutely certain it will pay off. This means doing more than just reading the content and hoping you can remember it on test day. It's important to make every minute of study count. There are two main areas you can focus on to make your studying count.

## Retention

It doesn't matter how much time you study if you can't remember the material. You need to make sure you are retaining the concepts. To check your retention of the information you're learning, try recalling it at later times with minimal prompting. Try carrying around flashcards and glance at one or two from time to time or ask a friend who's also studying for the test to quiz you.

To enhance your retention, look for ways to put the information into practice so that you can apply it rather than simply recalling it. If you're using the information in practical ways, it will be much easier to remember. Similarly, it helps to solidify a concept in your mind if you're not only reading it to yourself but also explaining it to someone else. Ask a friend to let you teach them about a concept you're a little shaky on (or speak aloud to an imaginary audience if necessary). As you try to summarize, define, give examples, and answer your friend's questions, you'll understand the concepts better and they will stay with you longer. Finally, step back for a big picture view and ask yourself how each piece of information fits with the whole subject. When you link the different concepts together and see them working together as a whole, it's easier to remember the individual components.

Finally, practice showing your work on any multi-step problems, even if you're just studying. Writing out each step you take to solve a problem will help solidify the process in your mind, and you'll be more likely to remember it during the test.

## Modality

*Modality* simply refers to the means or method by which you study. Choosing a study modality that fits your own individual learning style is crucial. No two people learn best in exactly the same way, so it's important to know your strengths and use them to your advantage.

For example, if you learn best by visualization, focus on visualizing a concept in your mind and draw an image or a diagram. Try color-coding your notes, illustrating them, or creating symbols that will trigger your mind to recall a learned concept. If you learn best by hearing or discussing information, find a study partner who learns the same way or read aloud to yourself. Think about how to put the information in your own words. Imagine that you are giving a lecture on the topic and record yourself so you can listen to it later.

For any learning style, flashcards can be helpful. Organize the information so you can take advantage of spare moments to review. Underline key words or phrases. Use different colors for different categories. Mnemonic devices (such as creating a short list in which every item starts with the same letter) can also help with retention. Find what works best for you and use it to store the information in your mind most effectively and easily.

# Strategy #3 – Practice the Right Way

Your success on test day depends not only on how many hours you put into preparing, but also on whether you prepared the right way. It's good to check along the way to see if your studying is paying off. One of the most effective ways to do this is by taking practice tests to evaluate your progress. Practice tests are useful because they show exactly where you need to improve. Every time you take a practice test, pay special attention to these three groups of questions:

- The questions you got wrong
- The questions you had to guess on, even if you guessed right
- The questions you found difficult or slow to work through

This will show you exactly what your weak areas are, and where you need to devote more study time. Ask yourself why each of these questions gave you trouble. Was it because you didn't understand the material? Was it because you didn't remember the vocabulary? Do you need more repetitions on this type of question to build speed and confidence? Dig into those questions and figure out how you can strengthen your weak areas as you go back to review the material.

Additionally, many practice tests have a section explaining the answer choices. It can be tempting to read the explanation and think that you now have a good understanding of the concept. However, an explanation likely only covers part of the question's broader context. Even if the explanation makes perfect sense, **go back and investigate** every concept related to the question until you're positive you have a thorough understanding.

As you go along, keep in mind that the practice test is just that: practice. Memorizing these questions and answers will not be very helpful on the actual test because it is unlikely to have any of the same exact questions. If you only know the right answers to the sample questions, you won't be prepared for the real thing. **Study the concepts** until you understand them fully, and then you'll be able to answer any question that shows up on the test.

It's important to wait on the practice tests until you're ready. If you take a test on your first day of study, you may be overwhelmed by the amount of material covered and how much you need to learn. Work up to it gradually.

On test day, you'll need to be prepared for answering questions, managing your time, and using the test-taking strategies you've learned. It's a lot to balance, like a mental marathon that will have a big impact on your future. Like training for a marathon, you'll need to start slowly and work your way up. When test day arrives, you'll be ready.

Start with the strategies you've read in the first two Success Strategies—plan your course and study in the way that works best for you. If you have time, consider using multiple study resources to get different approaches to the same concepts. It can be helpful to see difficult concepts from more than one angle. Then find a good source for practice tests. Many times, the test website will suggest potential study resources or provide sample tests.

# Practice Test Strategy

If you're able to find at least three practice tests, we recommend this strategy:

### Untimed and Open-Book Practice

Take the first test with no time constraints and with your notes and study guide handy. Take your time and focus on applying the strategies you've learned.

### Timed and Open-Book Practice

Take the second practice test open-book as well, but set a timer and practice pacing yourself to finish in time.

### Timed and Closed-Book Practice

Take any other practice tests as if it were test day. Set a timer and put away your study materials. Sit at a table or desk in a quiet room, imagine yourself at the testing center, and answer questions as quickly and accurately as possible.

Keep repeating timed and closed-book tests on a regular basis until you run out of practice tests or it's time for the actual test. Your mind will be ready for the schedule and stress of test day, and you'll be able to focus on recalling the material you've learned.

# Strategy #4 – Pace Yourself

Once you're fully prepared for the material on the test, your biggest challenge on test day will be managing your time. Just knowing that the clock is ticking can make you panic even if you have plenty of time left. Work on pacing yourself so you can build confidence against the time constraints of the exam. Pacing is a difficult skill to master, especially in a high-pressure environment, so **practice is vital**.

Set time expectations for your pace based on how much time is available. For example, if a section has 60 questions and the time limit is 30 minutes, you know you have to average 30 seconds or less per question in order to answer them all. Although 30 seconds is the hard limit, set 25 seconds per question as your goal, so you reserve extra time to spend on harder questions. When you budget extra time for the harder questions, you no longer have any reason to stress when those questions take longer to answer.

Don't let this time expectation distract you from working through the test at a calm, steady pace, but keep it in mind so you don't spend too much time on any one question. Recognize that taking extra time on one question you don't understand may keep you from answering two that you do understand later in the test. If your time limit for a question is up and you're still not sure of the answer, mark it and move on, and come back to it later if the time and the test format allow. If the testing format doesn't allow you to return to earlier questions, just make an educated guess; then put it out of your mind and move on.

On the easier questions, be careful not to rush. It may seem wise to hurry through them so you have more time for the challenging ones, but it's not worth missing one if you know the concept and just didn't take the time to read the question fully. Work efficiently but make sure you understand the question and have looked at all of the answer choices, since more than one may seem right at first.

Even if you're paying attention to the time, you may find yourself a little behind at some point. You should speed up to get back on track, but do so wisely. Don't panic; just take a few seconds less on each question until you're caught up. Don't guess without thinking, but do look through the answer choices and eliminate any you know are wrong. If you can get down to two choices, it is often worthwhile to guess from those. Once you've chosen an answer, move on and don't dwell on any that you skipped or had to hurry through. If a question was taking too long, chances are it was one of the harder ones, so you weren't as likely to get it right anyway.

On the other hand, if you find yourself getting ahead of schedule, it may be beneficial to slow down a little. The more quickly you work, the more likely you are to make a careless mistake that will affect your score. You've budgeted time for each question, so don't be afraid to spend that time. Practice an efficient but careful pace to get the most out of the time you have.

# Test-Taking Strategies

This section contains a list of test-taking strategies that you may find helpful as you work through the test. By taking what you know and applying logical thought, you can maximize your chances of answering any question correctly!

It is very important to realize that every question is different and every person is different: no single strategy will work on every question, and no single strategy will work for every person. That's why we've included all of them here, so you can try them out and determine which ones work best for different types of questions and which ones work best for you.

## Question Strategies

### ✓ Read Carefully

Read the question and the answer choices carefully. Don't miss the question because you misread the terms. You have plenty of time to read each question thoroughly and make sure you understand what is being asked. Yet a happy medium must be attained, so don't waste too much time. You must read carefully and efficiently.

### ✓ Contextual Clues

Look for contextual clues. If the question includes a word you are not familiar with, look at the immediate context for some indication of what the word might mean. Contextual clues can often give you all the information you need to decipher the meaning of an unfamiliar word. Even if you can't determine the meaning, you may be able to narrow down the possibilities enough to make a solid guess at the answer to the question.

### ✓ Prefixes

If you're having trouble with a word in the question or answer choices, try dissecting it. Take advantage of every clue that the word might include. Prefixes can be a huge help. Usually, they allow you to determine a basic meaning. *Pre-* means before, *post-* means after, *pro-* is positive, *de-* is negative. From prefixes, you can get an idea of the general meaning of the word and try to put it into context.

### ✓ Hedge Words

Watch out for critical hedge words, such as *likely, may, can, sometimes, often, almost, mostly, usually, generally, rarely,* and *sometimes.* Question writers insert these hedge phrases to cover every possibility. Often an answer choice will be wrong simply because it leaves no room for exception. Be on guard for answer choices that have definitive words such as *exactly* and *always.*

### ✓ Switchback Words

Stay alert for *switchbacks.* These are the words and phrases frequently used to alert you to shifts in thought. The most common switchback words are *but, although,* and *however.* Others include *nevertheless, on the other hand, even though, while, in spite of, despite,* and *regardless of.* Switchback words are important to catch because they can change the direction of the question or an answer choice.

### ⊘ Face Value

When in doubt, use common sense. Accept the situation in the problem at face value. Don't read too much into it. These problems will not require you to make wild assumptions. If you have to go beyond creativity and warp time or space in order to have an answer choice fit the question, then you should move on and consider the other answer choices. These are normal problems rooted in reality. The applicable relationship or explanation may not be readily apparent, but it is there for you to figure out. Use your common sense to interpret anything that isn't clear.

## Answer Choice Strategies

### ⊘ Answer Selection

The most thorough way to pick an answer choice is to identify and eliminate wrong answers until only one is left, then confirm it is the correct answer. Sometimes an answer choice may immediately seem right, but be careful. The test writers will usually put more than one reasonable answer choice on each question, so take a second to read all of them and make sure that the other choices are not equally obvious. As long as you have time left, it is better to read every answer choice than to pick the first one that looks right without checking the others.

### ⊘ Answer Choice Families

An answer choice family consists of two (in rare cases, three) answer choices that are very similar in construction and cannot all be true at the same time. If you see two answer choices that are direct opposites or parallels, one of them is usually the correct answer. For instance, if one answer choice says that quantity $x$ increases and another either says that quantity $x$ decreases (opposite) or says that quantity $y$ increases (parallel), then those answer choices would fall into the same family. An answer choice that doesn't match the construction of the answer choice family is more likely to be incorrect. Most questions will not have answer choice families, but when they do appear, you should be prepared to recognize them.

### ⊘ Eliminate Answers

Eliminate answer choices as soon as you realize they are wrong, but make sure you consider all possibilities. If you are eliminating answer choices and realize that the last one you are left with is also wrong, don't panic. Start over and consider each choice again. There may be something you missed the first time that you will realize on the second pass.

### ⊘ Avoid Fact Traps

Don't be distracted by an answer choice that is factually true but doesn't answer the question. You are looking for the choice that answers the question. Stay focused on what the question is asking for so you don't accidentally pick an answer that is true but incorrect. Always go back to the question and make sure the answer choice you've selected actually answers the question and is not merely a true statement.

### ⊘ Extreme Statements

In general, you should avoid answers that put forth extreme actions as standard practice or proclaim controversial ideas as established fact. An answer choice that states the "process should be used in certain situations, if…" is much more likely to be correct than one that states the "process should be discontinued completely." The first is a calm rational statement and doesn't even make a definitive, uncompromising stance, using a hedge word *if* to provide wiggle room, whereas the second choice is far more extreme.

### ✓ BENCHMARK

As you read through the answer choices and you come across one that seems to answer the question well, mentally select that answer choice. This is not your final answer, but it's the one that will help you evaluate the other answer choices. The one that you selected is your benchmark or standard for judging each of the other answer choices. Every other answer choice must be compared to your benchmark. That choice is correct until proven otherwise by another answer choice beating it. If you find a better answer, then that one becomes your new benchmark. Once you've decided that no other choice answers the question as well as your benchmark, you have your final answer.

### ✓ PREDICT THE ANSWER

Before you even start looking at the answer choices, it is often best to try to predict the answer. When you come up with the answer on your own, it is easier to avoid distractions and traps because you will know exactly what to look for. The right answer choice is unlikely to be word-for-word what you came up with, but it should be a close match. Even if you are confident that you have the right answer, you should still take the time to read each option before moving on.

## General Strategies

### ✓ TOUGH QUESTIONS

If you are stumped on a problem or it appears too hard or too difficult, don't waste time. Move on! Remember though, if you can quickly check for obviously incorrect answer choices, your chances of guessing correctly are greatly improved. Before you completely give up, at least try to knock out a couple of possible answers. Eliminate what you can and then guess at the remaining answer choices before moving on.

### ✓ CHECK YOUR WORK

Since you will probably not know every term listed and the answer to every question, it is important that you get credit for the ones that you do know. Don't miss any questions through careless mistakes. If at all possible, try to take a second to look back over your answer selection and make sure you've selected the correct answer choice and haven't made a costly careless mistake (such as marking an answer choice that you didn't mean to mark). This quick double check should more than pay for itself in caught mistakes for the time it costs.

### ✓ PACE YOURSELF

It's easy to be overwhelmed when you're looking at a page full of questions; your mind is confused and full of random thoughts, and the clock is ticking down faster than you would like. Calm down and maintain the pace that you have set for yourself. Especially as you get down to the last few minutes of the test, don't let the small numbers on the clock make you panic. As long as you are on track by monitoring your pace, you are guaranteed to have time for each question.

### ✓ DON'T RUSH

It is very easy to make errors when you are in a hurry. Maintaining a fast pace in answering questions is pointless if it makes you miss questions that you would have gotten right otherwise. Test writers like to include distracting information and wrong answers that seem right. Taking a little extra time to avoid careless mistakes can make all the difference in your test score. Find a pace that allows you to be confident in the answers that you select.

### ⊘ KEEP MOVING

Panicking will not help you pass the test, so do your best to stay calm and keep moving. Taking deep breaths and going through the answer elimination steps you practiced can help to break through a stress barrier and keep your pace.

## Final Notes

The combination of a solid foundation of content knowledge and the confidence that comes from practicing your plan for applying that knowledge is the key to maximizing your performance on test day. As your foundation of content knowledge is built up and strengthened, you'll find that the strategies included in this chapter become more and more effective in helping you quickly sift through the distractions and traps of the test to isolate the correct answer.

Now that you're preparing to move forward into the test content chapters of this book, be sure to keep your goal in mind. As you read, think about how you will be able to apply this information on the test. If you've already seen sample questions for the test and you have an idea of the question format and style, try to come up with questions of your own that you can answer based on what you're reading. This will give you valuable practice applying your knowledge in the same ways you can expect to on test day.

**Good luck and good studying!**

# Global History

## World History Pre-1400

### Different Periods of Prehistory

Prehistory is the period of human history before writing was developed. The three major periods of prehistory are:

- **Lower Paleolithic**—Humans used crude tools.
- **Upper Paleolithic**—Humans began to develop a wider variety of tools. These tools were better made and more specialized. They also began to wear clothes, organize in groups with definite social structures, and practice art. Most lived in caves during this time period.
- **Neolithic**—Social structures became even more complex, including the growth of a sense of family and the ideas of religion and government. Humans learned to domesticate animals and produce crops, build houses, start fires with friction tools, and to knit, spin and weave.

### Anthropology

Anthropology is the study of human culture. Anthropologists study groups of humans, how they relate to each other, and the similarities and differences between these different groups and cultures. Anthropological research takes two approaches: **cross-cultural research** and **comparative research**. Most anthropologists work by living among different cultures and participating in those cultures in order to learn about them.

There are four major **divisions** within anthropology:

- Biological anthropology
- Cultural anthropology
- Linguistic anthropology
- Archaeology

### Science of Archaeology

Archaeology is the study of past human cultures by evaluating what they leave behind. This can include bones, buildings, art, tools, pottery, graves, and even trash. Archaeologists maintain detailed notes and records of their findings and use special tools to evaluate what they find. Photographs, notes, maps, artifacts, and surveys of the area can all contribute to the evaluation of an archaeological site. By studying all these elements of numerous archeological sites, scientists have been able to theorize that humans or near-humans have existed for about 600,000 years. Before that, more primitive humans are believed to have appeared about one million years ago. These humans eventually developed into **Cro-Magnon man**, and then **Homo sapiens**, or modern man.

### Human Development from the Lower Paleolithic to the Iron Age

Human development has been divided into several phases:

- **Lower Paleolithic or Early Stone Age**, beginning two to three million years ago—early humans used tools like needles, hatchets, awls, and cutting tools.
- **Middle Paleolithic or Middle Stone Age**, beginning approximately 300,000 BC—sophisticated stone tools were developed, along with hunting, gathering, and ritual practices.

- **Upper Paleolithic or Late Stone Age**, beginning approximately 40,000 BC—including the Mesolithic and Neolithic eras, textiles and pottery were developed. Humans of this era discovered the wheel, began to practice agriculture, made polished tools, and had some domesticated animals.
- **Bronze Age**, beginning approximately 3000 BC—metals are discovered and the first civilizations emerge as humans become more technologically advanced.
- **Iron Age**, beginning 1200 to 1000 BC—metal tools replace stone tools as humans develop knowledge of smelting.

## Requirements for Civilization and State Where the Earliest Civilizations Developed

Civilizations are defined as having the following characteristics:

- Use of metal to make weapons and tools
- Written language
- A defined territorial state
- A calendar

The **earliest civilizations** developed in river valleys where reliable, fertile land was easily found, including:

- The Nile River Valley in Egypt
- Mesopotamia
- The Indus Valley
- Hwang Ho in China

The very earliest civilizations developed in the **Tigris-Euphrates valley** in Mesopotamia, which is now part of Iraq, and in Egypt's **Nile valley**. These civilizations arose between 5000 and 3000 BC. The area where these civilizations grew is known as the Fertile Crescent. Geography and the availability of water made large-scale human habitation possible.

## Importance of Rivers and Water to the Growth of Early Civilizations

The earliest civilizations are also referred to as **fluvial civilizations** because they were founded near rivers. Rivers and the water they provide were vital to these early groupings, offering:

- Water for drinking, cultivating crops, and caring for domesticated animals
- A gathering place for wild animals that could be hunted
- Rich soil deposits as a result of regular flooding

**Irrigation techniques** helped direct water where it was most needed, to sustain herds of domestic animals and to nourish crops of increasing size and quality.

## Fertile Crescent

**James Breasted**, an archaeologist from the University of Chicago, popularized the term "**Fertile Crescent**" to describe the area in Southwest Asia and the Mediterranean basin where the earliest civilizations arose. The region includes modern-day Iraq, Syria, Lebanon, Israel, Palestine, and Jordan. It is bordered on the south by the Syrian and Arabian Deserts, the west by the Mediterranean Sea, and to the north and east by the Taurus and Zagros Mountains, respectively. This area not only provided the raw materials for the development of increasingly advanced civilizations but also saw waves of migration and invasion, leading to the earliest wars and genocides as groups conquered and absorbed each other's cultures and inhabitants.

## Accomplishments of the Egyptian, Sumerian, Babylonian, and Assyrian Cultures

The **Egyptians** were one of the most advanced ancient cultures, having developed construction methods to build the great pyramids, as well as a form of writing known as hieroglyphics. Their religion was highly developed and complex and included advanced techniques for the preservation of bodies after death. They also made paper by processing papyrus, a plant commonly found along the Nile, invented the decimal system, devised a solar calendar, and advanced overall knowledge of mathematics.

The **Sumerians** were the first to invent the wheel, and also brought irrigation systems into use. Their cuneiform writing was simpler than Egyptian hieroglyphs, and they developed the timekeeping system we still use today.

The **Babylonians** are best known for the Code of Hammurabi, an advanced law code.

The **Assyrians** developed horse-drawn chariots and an organized military.

## Accomplishments of the Hebrew, Persian, Minoan, and Mycenaean Cultures

The **Hebrew** or ancient Israelite culture developed the monotheistic religion that eventually developed into modern Judaism and Christianity.

The **Persians** were conquerors, but those they conquered were allowed to keep their own laws, customs, and religious traditions rather than being forced to accept those of their conquerors. They also developed an alphabet and practiced Zoroastrianism and Mithraism, religions that have influenced modern religious practice.

The **Minoans** used a syllabic writing system and built large, colorful palaces. These ornate buildings included sewage systems, running water, bathtubs, and even flushing toilets. Their script, known as Linear A, has yet to be deciphered.

The **Mycenaeans** practiced a religion that grew into the Greek pantheon, worshipping Zeus and other Olympian gods. They developed Linear B, a writing system used to write the earliest known form of Greek.

## Phoenicians and Early Culture in India and Ancient China

Skilled seafarers and navigators, the Phoenicians used the stars to navigate their ships at night. They developed a purple dye that was in great demand in the ancient world, and worked with glass and metals. They also devised a phonetic alphabet, using symbols to represent individual sounds rather than whole words or syllables.

The Indus Valley Civilization (IVC) was an urban civilization arose in the Indus Valley, located in between the modern countries of Iran, India, and Pakistan. These ancient humans developed the concept of zero in mathematics, practiced an early form of the Hindu religion, and developed the caste system which is still prevalent in India today. Archeologists are still uncovering information about this highly developed ancient civilization.

In ancient **China**, human civilization developed along the **Yangtze River**. These people produced silk, grew millet, and made pottery, including Longshan black pottery.

## Civilizations of Mesopotamia

The major civilizations of Mesopotamia, in what is now called the **Middle East**, were:

- Sumerians
- Amorites
- Hittites
- Assyrians
- Chaldeans
- Persians

These cultures controlled different areas of Mesopotamia during various time periods but were similar in that they were **autocratic**: a single ruler served as the head of the government and often was the main religious ruler as well. These rulers were often tyrannical, militaristic leaders who controlled all aspects of life, including law, trade, and religious activity. Portions of the legacies of these civilizations remain in cultures today. These include mythologies, religious systems, mathematical innovations, and even elements of various languages.

## Sumerians

Sumer, located in the southern part of Mesopotamia, consisted of a dozen **city-states**. Each city-state had its own gods, and the leader of each city-state also served as the high priest. Cultural legacies of Sumer include:

- The invention of writing
- The invention of the wheel
- The first library—established in Assyria by Ashurbanipal
- The Hanging Gardens of Babylon—one of the Seven Wonders of the Ancient World
- First written laws—Ur-Nammu's Codes and the Codes of Hammurabi
- The *Epic of Gilgamesh*—the first recorded epic story

**Review Video: How was Sumerian Culture Spread Throughout Mesopotamia?**
Visit mometrix.com/academy and enter code: 939880

## Kushites

Kush, or Cush, was located in Nubia, south of ancient Egypt, and the earliest existing records of this civilization were found in Egyptian texts. At one time, Kush was the largest empire on the Nile River, ruling not only Nubia but Upper and Lower Egypt as well.

In Neolithic times, Kushites lived in villages, with buildings made of mud bricks. They were settled rather than nomadic and practiced hunting and fishing, cultivated grain, and also herded cattle. **Kerma**, the capital, was a major center of trade.

Kush determined leadership through **matrilineal descent** of their kings, as did Egypt. Their heads of state, the Kandake or Kentake, were female. Their polytheistic religion included the primary Egyptian gods as well as regional gods, including a lion-headed god, which is commonly found in African cultures.

Kush was conquered by the **Aksumite Empire** in the 4th century AD.

### Minoans

The Minoans lived on the island of Crete, just off the coast of Greece. This civilization reigned from approximately 4000 to 1400 BC and is considered to be the first advanced civilization in Europe. The Minoans developed writing systems known to linguists as **Linear A** and **Linear B**. Linear A has not yet been translated; Linear B evolved into classical Greek script. "Minoans" is not the name they used for themselves but is instead a variation on the name of King Minos, a king in Greek mythology believed by some to have been a denizen of Crete. The Minoan civilization subsisted on trade, and their way of life was often disrupted by earthquakes and volcanoes. Much is still unknown about the Minoans, and archaeologists continue to study their architecture and archaeological remains. The Minoan culture eventually fell to Greek invaders and was supplanted by the **Mycenaean civilization**.

### Ancient India

The civilizations of ancient India gave rise to both **Hinduism** and **Buddhism**, major world religions that have influenced countries far from their place of origin. Practices such as yoga, increasingly popular in the West, can trace their roots to these earliest Indian civilizations, and the poses are still formally referred to by Sanskrit names. Literature from ancient India includes the *Mahabharata* containing the *Bhagavad Gita*, the *Ramayana*, *Arthashastra*, and the *Vedas*, a collection of sacred texts. Indo-European languages, including English, find their beginnings in these ancient cultures. Ancient Indo-Aryan languages such as Sanskrit are still used in some formal Hindu practices.

### Earliest Civilizations in China

Many historians believe **Chinese civilization** is the oldest uninterrupted civilization in the world. The **Neolithic age** in China goes back to 10,000 BC, with agriculture in China beginning as early as 5000 BC. Their system of writing dates to 1500 BC. The Yellow River served as the center for the earliest Chinese settlements. In Ningxia, in northwest China, there are carvings on cliffs that date back to the Paleolithic Period, indicating the extreme antiquity of Chinese culture. Literature from ancient China includes Confucius' *Analects*, the *Tao Te Ching*, and a variety of poetry.

### Ancient Cultures in the Americas

Less is known of ancient American civilizations since less was left behind. Some of the more well-known cultures include:

- The **Norte Chico civilization** in Peru, an agricultural society of up to 30 individual communities, existed over 5,000 years ago. This culture is also known as the Caral-Supe civilization, and is the oldest known civilization in the Americas.
- The **Anasazi**, or Ancestral Pueblo People, lived in what is now the southwestern United States. Emerging about 1200 BC, the Anasazi built complex adobe dwellings and were the forerunners of later Pueblo Indian cultures.
- The **Maya** emerged in southern Mexico and northern Central America as early as 2600 BC. They developed a written language and a complex calendar.

### Mycenaeans

In contrast to the Minoans, whom they displaced, the **Mycenaeans** relied more on conquest than on trade. Mycenaean states included Sparta, Athens, and Corinth. The history of this civilization, including the **Trojan War**, was recorded by the Greek poet **Homer**. His work was largely considered mythical until archaeologists discovered evidence of the city of **Troy** in Hisarlik, Turkey. Archaeologists continue to add to the body of information about this ancient culture, translating documents written in Linear B, a script derived from the Minoan Linear A. It is theorized that the

Mycenaean civilization was eventually destroyed in either a Dorian invasion or an attack by Greek invaders from the north.

### Dorian Invasion

A Dorian invasion does not refer to an invasion by a particular group of people, but rather is a hypothetical theory to explain the end of the **Mycenaean civilization** and the growth of **classical Greece**. Ancient tradition refers to these events as "the return of the Heracleidae," or the sons (descendants) of Hercules. Archaeologists and historians still do not know exactly who conquered the Mycenaeans, but it is believed to have occurred around 1200 BC, contemporaneous with the destruction of the **Hittite civilization** in what is now modern Turkey. The Hittites speak of an attack by people of the Aegean Sea, or the "Sea People." Only Athens was left intact.

### Spartans vs. Athenians

Both powerful city-states, Sparta and Athens fought each other in the **Peloponnesian War** (431-404 BC). Despite their proximity, the Spartans and the Athenians nurtured contrasting cultures:

- The **Spartans**, located in Peloponnesus, were ruled by an oligarchic military state. They practiced farming, disallowed trade for Spartan citizens, and valued military arts and strict discipline. They emerged as the strongest military force in the area and maintained this status for many years. In one memorable encounter, a small group of Spartans held off a huge army of Persians at Thermopylae.
- The **Athenians** were centered in Attica, where the land was rocky and unsuitable for farming. Like the Spartans, they descended from invaders who spoke Greek. Their government was very different from Sparta's; it was in Athens that democracy was created by Cleisthenes of Athens in 508 BC. Athenians excelled in art, theater, architecture, and philosophy.

### Contributions of Ancient Greece that Still Exist Today

Ancient Greece made numerous major contributions to cultural development, including:

- **Theater**—Aristophanes and other Greek playwrights laid the groundwork for modern theatrical performance.
- **Alphabet**—the Greek alphabet, derived from the Phoenician alphabet, developed into the Roman alphabet, and then into our modern-day alphabet.
- **Geometry**—Pythagoras and Euclid pioneered much of the system of geometry still taught today. Archimedes made various mathematical discoveries, including calculating a very accurate value of pi.
- **Historical writing**—much of ancient history doubles as mythology or religious texts. Herodotus and Thucydides made use of research and interpretation to record historical events.
- **Philosophy**—Socrates, Plato, and Aristotle served as the fathers of Western philosophy. Their work is still required reading for philosophy students.

**Review Video: Ancient Greece Timeline**
Visit mometrix.com/academy and enter code: 800829

### Alexander the Great

Born to Philip II of Macedon and tutored by Aristotle, **Alexander the Great** is considered one of the greatest conquerors in history. He conquered Egypt and the Achaemenid/Persian Empire, a powerful empire founded by Cyrus the Great that spanned three continents, and he traveled as far as India and the Iberian Peninsula. Though Alexander died from malaria at age 32, his conquering efforts spread **Greek culture** into the east. This cultural diffusion left a greater mark on history than did his empire, which fell apart due to internal conflict not long after his death. Trade between the East and West increased, as did an exchange of ideas and beliefs that influenced both regions greatly. The **Hellenistic traditions** his conquest spread were prevalent in Byzantine culture until as late as the 15th century.

## HITTITES

The Hittites were centered in what is now Turkey, but their empire extended into Palestine and Syria. They conquered the Babylonian civilization, but adopted their religion, laws, and literature. Overall, the Hittites tended to tolerate other religions, unlike many other contemporary cultures, and absorbed foreign gods into their own belief systems rather than forcing their religion onto peoples they conquered. The **Hittite Empire** reached its peak in 1600-1200 BC. After a war with Egypt, which weakened them severely, they were eventually conquered by the **Assyrians**.

## PERSIAN WARS

The Persian Empire, ruled by **Cyrus the Great**, encompassed an area from the Black Sea to Afghanistan and beyond into Central Asia. After the death of Cyrus, **Darius I** became king in 522 BC. The empire reached its zenith during his reign, and Darius attempted to conquer Greece as well. From 499 to 449 BC, the Greeks and Persians fought in the **Persian Wars**. The **Peace of Callias** brought an end to the fighting, after the Greeks were able to repel the invasion.

Battles of the Persian Wars included:

- The **Battle of Marathon**—heavily outnumbered Greek forces managed to achieve victory.
- The **Battle of Thermopylae**—a small band of Spartans held off a throng of Persian troops for several days before Persia defeated the Greeks and captured an evacuated Athens.
- The **Battle of Salamis**—this was a naval battle that again saw outnumbered Greeks achieving victory.
- The **Battle of Plataea**—this was another Greek victory, but one in which they outnumbered the Persians. This ended the invasion of Greece.

## MAURYA EMPIRE

The Maurya Empire was a large, powerful empire established in India. It was one of the largest ever to rule in the Indian subcontinent and existed from 322 to 185 BC, ruled by **Chandragupta Maurya** after the withdrawal from India of Alexander the Great. The Maurya Empire was highly developed, including a standardized economic system, waterways, and private corporations. Trade to the Greeks and others became common, with goods including silk, exotic foods, and spices. Religious development included the rise of Buddhism and Jainism. The laws of the Maurya Empire protected not only civil and social rights of the citizens, but they also protected animals, establishing protected zones for economically important creatures such as elephants, lions, and tigers. This period of time in Indian history was largely peaceful, perhaps due to the strong Buddhist beliefs of many of its leaders. The empire finally fell after a succession of weak leaders and was taken over by **Demetrius**, a Greco-Bactrian king who took advantage of this lapse in leadership to conquer southern Afghanistan and Pakistan around 180 BC, forming the **Indo-Greek Kingdom**.

## Development and Growth of the Chinese Empires

In China, history was divided into a series of **dynasties**. The most famous of these, the **Han dynasty**, existed from 206 BC to AD 220. Accomplishments of the Chinese empires included:

- Building the Great Wall of China
- Numerous inventions, including paper, paper money, printing, and gunpowder
- High level of artistic development
- Silk production

The Chinese dynasties were comparable to Rome as far as their artistic and intellectual accomplishments, as well as the size and scope of their influence.

## Roman Empire and Republic

Rome began humbly, in a single town that grew out of Etruscan settlements and traditions, founded, according to legend, by twin brothers Romulus and Remus, who were raised by wolves. Romulus killed Remus, and from his legacy grew Rome. A thousand years later, the **Roman Empire** covered a significant portion of the known world, from what is now Scotland, across Europe, and into the Middle East. **Hellenization**, or the spread of Greek culture throughout the world, served as an inspiration and a model for the spread of Roman culture. Rome brought in belief systems of conquered peoples as well as their technological and scientific accomplishments, melding the disparate parts into a Roman core. Rome began as a **republic** ruled by consuls, but after the assassination of **Julius Caesar**, it became an **empire** led by emperors. Rome's overall government was autocratic, but local officials came from the provinces where they lived. This limited administrative system was probably a major factor in the long life of the empire.

**Review Video: Roman Republic Part One**
Visit mometrix.com/academy and enter code: 360192

**Review Video: Roman Republic Part Two**
Visit mometrix.com/academy and enter code: 881514

## Development of the Byzantine Empire from the Roman Empire

In the early 4th century, the Roman Empire split, with the eastern portion becoming the Eastern Empire, or the **Byzantine Empire**. In AD 330, **Constantine** founded the city of **Constantinople**, which became the center of the Byzantine Empire. Its major influences came from Mesopotamia and Persia, in contrast to the Western Empire, which maintained traditions more closely linked to Greece and Carthage. Byzantium's position gave it an advantage over invaders from the West and the East, as well as control over trade from both regions. It protected the Western empire from invasion from the Persians and the Ottomans, and practiced a more centralized rule than in the West. The Byzantines were famous for lavish art and architecture, as well as the Code of Justinian, which collected Roman law into a clear system. The Byzantine Empire finally fell to the **Ottomans** in 1453.

## Significance of the Nicene Creed

The **Byzantine Empire** was Christian-based but incorporated Greek language, philosophy, and literature and drew its law and government policies from Rome. However, there was as yet no unified doctrine of Christianity, as it was a relatively new religion that had spread rapidly and without a great deal of organization. In 325, the **First Council of Nicaea** addressed this issue. From this conference came the **Nicene Creed**, addressing the Trinity and other basic Christian beliefs. The **Council of Chalcedon** in 451 further defined the view of the Trinity.

## Factors that Led to the Fall of the Western Roman Empire

**Germanic tribes**, including the Visigoths, Ostrogoths, Vandals, Saxons, and Franks, controlled most of Europe. The Roman Empire faced major opposition on that front. The increasing size of the empire also made it harder to manage, leading to dissatisfaction throughout the empire as Roman government became less efficient. Germanic tribes refused to adhere to the Nicene Creed, instead following **Arianism**, which led the Roman Catholic Church to declare them heretics. The **Franks** proved a powerful military force in their defeat of the Muslims in 732. In 768, **Charlemagne** became king of the Franks. These tribes waged several wars against Rome, including the invasion of Britannia by the Angles and Saxons. Far-flung Rome lost control over this area of its empire, and eventually, Rome itself was **invaded**.

## Iconoclasm and the Conflict Between the Roman Catholic and Eastern Orthodox Churches

**Emperor Leo III** ordered the destruction of all icons throughout the Byzantine Empire. Images of Jesus were replaced with crosses, and images of Jesus, Mary, or other religious figures were considered blasphemy on the grounds of idolatry. **Pope Gregory II** called a synod to discuss the issue. The synod declared that the images were not heretical and that strong disciplinary measures would result for anyone who destroyed them. Leo's response was an attempt to kill Pope Gregory, but this plan ended in failure.

## Effect of the Viking Invasions on the Culture of England and Europe

Vikings invaded Northern France in the 10th century, eventually becoming the **Normans**. Originating in Scandinavia, the **Vikings** were accomplished seafarers with advanced knowledge of trade routes. With overpopulation plaguing their native lands, they began to travel. From the 8th to the 11th centuries, they spread throughout Europe, conquering and colonizing. Vikings invaded and colonized England in several waves, including the **Anglo-Saxon invasions** that displaced Roman control. Their influence remained significant in England, affecting everything from the language of the country to place names and even the government and social structure. By 900, Vikings had settled in **Iceland**. They proceeded then to **Greenland** and eventually to **North America**, arriving in the New World even before the Spanish and British who claimed the lands several centuries later. They also traded with the Byzantine Empire until the 11th century, when their significant level of activity came to an end.

## West vs. East 10th-Century Events

In **Europe**, the years AD 500-1000 are largely known as the **Dark Ages**. In the 10th century, numerous Viking invasions disrupted societies that had been more settled under Roman rule. Vikings settled in Northern France, eventually becoming the Normans. By the 11th century, Europe would rise again into the **High Middle Ages** with the beginning of the **Crusades**.

In **China**, wars also raged. This led the Chinese to make use of gunpowder for the first time in warfare.

In the **Americas**, the **Mayan Empire** was winding down while the **Toltec** became more prominent. **Pueblo** Indian culture was also at its zenith.

In the **East**, the **Muslims** and the **Byzantine Empire** were experiencing a significant period of growth and development.

# World History 1400 to 1914

## Feudalism in Europe in the Middle Ages

A major element of the social and economic life of Europe, **feudalism** developed as a way to ensure European rulers would have the wherewithal to quickly raise an army when necessary. **Vassals** swore loyalty and promised to provide military service for lords, who in return offered a **fief**, or a parcel of land, for them to use to generate their livelihood. Vassals could work the land themselves, have it worked by **peasants** or **serfs**—workers who had few rights and were little more than slaves—or grant the fief to someone else. The king legally owned all the land, but in return, promised to protect the vassals from invasion and war. Vassals returned a certain percentage of their income to the lords, who in turn, passed a portion of their income on to the king. A similar practice was **manorialism**, in which the feudal system was applied to a self-contained manor. These manors were often owned by the lords who ran them but were usually included in the same system of loyalty and promises of protection that drove feudalism.

**Review Video: The Middle Ages: Feudalism**
Visit mometrix.com/academy and enter code: 165907

## Effect of Black Death on Medieval Politics and Economic Conditions

The Black Death, believed to be **bubonic plague**, most likely came to Europe on fleas carried by rats on sailing vessels. The plague killed more than a third of the entire population of Europe and effectively ended **feudalism** as a political system. Many who had formerly served as peasants or serfs found different work, as a demand for skilled labor grew. Nation-states grew in power, and in the face of the pandemic, many began to turn away from faith in God and toward the ideals of ancient Greece and Rome for government and other beliefs.

**Review Video: Black Death (An Overview)**
Visit mometrix.com/academy and enter code: 431857

## Influence of the Roman Catholic Church Over Medieval Society

The Roman Catholic Church extended significant influence both politically and economically throughout medieval society. The church supplied **education**, as there were no established schools or universities. To a large extent, the church had filled a power void left by various invasions throughout the former Roman Empire, leading it to exercise a role that was far more **political** than religious. Kings were heavily influenced by the pope and other church officials, and churches controlled large amounts of land throughout Europe.

## Progression of the Crusades and Major Figures Involved

The Crusades began in the 11th century and continued into the 15th. The major goal of these various military ventures was to slow the progression of Muslim forces into Europe and to expel them from the **Holy Land**, where they had taken control of Jerusalem and Palestine. Alexius I, the Byzantine emperor, called for help from **Pope Urban** II when Palestine was taken. In 1095, the pope, hoping to reunite Eastern and Western Christianity, encouraged all Christians to help the cause. Amidst great bloodshed, this crusade recaptured **Jerusalem**, but over the next centuries, Jerusalem and other areas of the Holy Land changed hands numerous times. The **Second Crusade** (1147-1149) consisted of an unsuccessful attempt to retake Damascus. The **Third Crusade**, under Pope Gregory VIII, attempted to recapture Jerusalem but failed. The **Fourth Crusade**, under Pope Innocent III, attempted to come into the Holy Land via Egypt. The Crusades led to greater power for the pope and the Catholic Church in general and also opened numerous trading and cultural routes between Europe and the East.

## Political Developments in India Through the 11th Century

After the Mauryan dynasty, the **Guptas** ruled India, maintaining a long period of peace and prosperity in the area. During this time, the Indian people invented the decimal system and the concept of zero. They produced cotton and calico, as well as other products in high demand in Europe and Asia, and developed a complex system of medicine. The Gupta Dynasty ended in the 6th century. First, the **Huns** invaded, and then the **Hephthalites** (an Asian nomadic tribe) destroyed the weakened empire. In the 14th century, **Tamerlane**, a Muslim who envisioned restoring Genghis Khan's empire, expanded India's borders and founded the **Mogul Empire**. His grandson Akbar promoted freedom of religion and built a widespread number of mosques, forts, and other buildings throughout the country.

## Development of Chinese and Japanese Governments Through the 11th Century

After the Mongols, led by Genghis Khan and his grandson Kublai Khan, unified the Mongol Empire, **China** was led by the **Ming Dynasty** (1368-1644) and the **Manchu (also known as Qing) Dynasty** (1644-1912). Both dynasties were isolationist, ending China's interaction with other countries until the 18th century. The Ming Dynasty was known for its porcelain, while the Manchus focused on farming and road construction as the population grew.

**Japan** developed independently of China but borrowed the Buddhist religion, the Chinese writing system, and other elements of Chinese society. Ruled by the divine emperor, Japan basically functioned on a feudal system led by **daimyo**, or warlords, and soldiers known as **samurai**. Japan remained isolationist, not interacting significantly with the rest of the world until the 1800s.

## Ming Dynasty

The Ming dynasty lasted in China from AD 1368 to 1644. This dynasty was established by a Buddhist monk, **Zhu Yuanzhang**, who quickly became obsessed with consolidating power in the central government and was known for the brutality with which he achieved his ends. It was during the **Ming dynasty** that China developed and introduced its famous civil service examinations, rigorous tests on the **Confucian classics**. The future of an ambitious Chinese youth depended on his performance on this exam. The capital was transferred from Nanjing to Beijing during this period, and the **Forbidden City** was constructed inside the new capital. The Ming period, despite its constant expansionary wars, also continued China's artistic resurgence; the porcelain of this period is especially admired.

## Developments in Africa Through the 11th Century

Much of Africa was difficult to traverse early on, due to the large amount of desert and other inhospitable terrain. **Egypt** remained important, though most of the northern coast became Muslim as their armies spread through the area. **Ghana** rose as a trade center in the 9th century, lasting into the 12th century, primarily trading in gold, which it exchanged for Saharan salt. **Mali** rose somewhat later, with the trade center Timbuktu becoming an important exporter of goods such as iron, leather, and tin. Mali also dealt in agricultural trade, becoming one of the most significant trading centers in West Africa. The Muslim religion dominated, and technological advancement was sparse.

African culture was largely defined through migration, as Arab merchants and others settled on the continent, particularly along the east coast. Scholars from the Muslim nations gravitated to

Timbuktu, which in addition to its importance in trade, had also become a magnet for those seeking Islamic knowledge and education.

### History of Islam and Its Role in Bringing Unity to the Middle East

Born in AD 570, **Muhammad** began preaching around 613, leading his followers in a new religion called **Islam**, which means "submission to God's will." Before this time, the Arabian Peninsula was inhabited largely by Bedouins, nomads who battled amongst each other and lived in tribal organizations. But by the time Muhammad died in 632, most of Arabia had become Muslim to some extent.

Muhammad conquered **Mecca**, where a temple called the **Kaaba** had long served as a center of the nomadic religions. He declared this temple the most sacred of Islam, and Mecca as the holy city. His writings became the **Koran**, or **Qur'an**, divine revelations he said had been delivered to him by the angel Gabriel.

Muhammad's teachings gave the formerly tribal Arabian people a sense of unity that had not existed in the area before. After his death, the converted Muslims of Arabia conquered a vast territory, creating an empire and bringing advances in literature, technology, science, and art as Europe was declining under the scourge of the Black Death. Literature from this period includes the *Arabian Nights* and the *Rubaiyat* of Omar Khayyam.

Later in its development, Islam split into two factions; the **Shiite** and the **Sunni** Muslims. Conflict continues today between these groups.

### Ottoman Empire

By 1400, the Ottomans had grown in power in Anatolia and had begun attempts to take Constantinople. In 1453, they finally conquered the Byzantine capital and renamed it **Istanbul**. The **Ottoman Empire's** major strength, much like Rome before it, lay in its ability to unite widely disparate people through religious tolerance. This tolerance, which stemmed from the idea that Muslims, Christians, and Jews were fundamentally related and could coexist, enabled the Ottomans to develop a widely varied culture. They also believed in just laws and just government, with government centered in a monarch, known as the **sultan**.

### Renaissance

Renaissance literally means "rebirth." After the darkness of the Dark Ages and the Black Plague, interest rose again in the beliefs and politics of ancient Greece and Rome. Art, literature, music, science, and philosophy all burgeoned during the Renaissance.

Many of the ideas of the Renaissance began in **Florence, Italy** in the 14th century, spurred by the **Medici** family. Education for the upper classes expanded to include law, math, reading, writing, and classical Greek and Roman works. As the Renaissance progressed, the world was presented through art and literature in a realistic way that had never been explored before. This **realism** drove culture to new heights.

**Review Video: Renaissance**
Visit mometrix.com/academy and enter code: 123100

### Renaissance Artists, Authors, and Scientists

**Artists** of the Renaissance included Leonardo da Vinci, also an inventor; Michelangelo, also an architect; and others who focused on realism in their work. In **literature**, major contributions came from humanist authors like Petrarch, Erasmus, Sir Thomas More, and Boccaccio, who believed man should focus on reality rather than on the ethereal. Shakespeare, Cervantes, and Dante followed in their footsteps, and their works found a wide audience thanks to Gutenberg's development of the printing press.

**Scientific developments** of the Renaissance included the work of Copernicus, Galileo, and Kepler, who challenged the geocentric philosophies of the day by proving that the earth was not the center of the solar system.

## Two Phases of the Reformation Period

The Reformation consisted of both the Protestant and the Catholic Reformation. The **Protestant Reformation** rose in Germany when **Martin Luther** protested abuses of the Catholic Church. **John Calvin** led the movement in Switzerland, while in England, King Henry VIII made use of the Reformation's ideas to further his own political goals. The **Catholic Reformation**, or **Counter-Reformation**, occurred in response to the Protestant movement, leading to various changes in the Catholic Church. Some provided wider tolerance of different religious viewpoints, but others actually increased the persecution of those deemed to be heretics.

From a **religious** standpoint, the Reformation occurred due to abuses by the Catholic Church such as indulgences and dispensations, religious offices being offered up for sale, and an increasingly dissolute clergy. **Politically**, the Reformation was driven by increased power of various ruling monarchs, who wished to take all power to themselves rather than allowing power to remain with the church. They also had begun to chafe at papal taxes and the church's increasing wealth. The ideas of the Protestant Revolution removed power from the Catholic Church and the Pope himself, playing nicely into the hands of those monarchs, such as Henry VIII, who wanted out from under the church's control.

**Review Video: Martin Luther and the Reformation**
Visit mometrix.com/academy and enter code: 691828

**Review Video: What was the Counter-Reformation?**
Visit mometrix.com/academy and enter code: 950498

**Review Video: Who Were the Protestants?**
Visit mometrix.com/academy and enter code: 583582

## Developments of the Scientific Revolution

In addition to holding power in the political realm, church doctrine also governed scientific belief. During the **Scientific Revolution**, astronomers and other scientists began to amass evidence that challenged the church's scientific doctrines. Major figures of the Scientific Revolution included:

- **Nicolaus Copernicus**—wrote *On the Revolutions of the Celestial Spheres*, arguing that the earth revolved around the sun
- **Tycho Brahe**—cataloged astronomical observations
- **Johannes Kepler**—developed laws of planetary motion
- **Galileo Galilei**—defended the heliocentric theories of Copernicus and Kepler, discovered four moons of Jupiter, and died under house arrest by the church, charged with heresy
- **Isaac Newton**—discovered gravity; studied optics, calculus, and physics; and believed the workings of nature could be studied and proven through observation

**Review Video: The Scientific Revolution**
Visit mometrix.com/academy and enter code: 974600

## Major Ideas of the Enlightenment

During the Enlightenment, philosophers and scientists began to rely more and more on **observation** to support their ideas rather than building on past beliefs, particularly those held by the church. A focus on **ethics and logic** drove their work. Major philosophers of the **Enlightenment** included:

- **Rene Descartes**—he famously wrote, "I think, therefore I am." He believed strongly in logic and rules of observation.
- **David Hume**—he pioneered empiricism and skepticism, believing that truth could only be found through direct experience and that what others said to be true was always suspect.
- **Immanuel Kant**—he believed in self-examination and observation and that the root of morality lay within human beings.
- **Jean-Jacques Rousseau**—he developed the idea of the social contract, that government existed by the agreement of the people, and that the government was obligated to protect the people and their basic rights. His ideas heavily influenced the founding fathers.

**Review Video: What was the Age of Enlightenment?**
Visit mometrix.com/academy and enter code: 143022

## American Revolution vs. French Revolution

Both the American and French Revolution came about as a protest against the excesses and overly controlling nature of their respective monarchs. In **America**, the British colonies had been left mostly to self-govern until the British monarchs began to increase control, spurring the colonies to revolt. In **France**, the nobility's excesses had led to increasingly difficult economic conditions, with inflation, heavy taxation, and food shortages creating great burdens on the lower classes. Both revolutions led to the development of republics to replace the monarchies that were displaced. However, the French Revolution eventually led to the rise of the dictator **Napoleon Bonaparte**, while the American Revolution produced a working **republic** from the beginning.

## Events and Figures of the French Revolution

In 1789, **King Louis XVI**, faced with a huge national debt, convened parliament. The **Third Estate**, or Commons, a division of the French parliament, then claimed power, and the king's resistance led to the storming of the **Bastille**, the royal prison. The people established a constitutional monarchy. When King Louis XVI and Marie Antoinette attempted to leave the country, they were executed on the guillotine. From 1793 to 1794, **Robespierre** and extreme radicals, the **Jacobins**, instituted a **Reign of Terror**, executing tens of thousands of nobles as well as anyone considered an enemy of the Revolution. Robespierre was then executed as well, and the **Directory** came into power, leading to a temporary return to bourgeois values. This governing body proved incompetent and corrupt, allowing **Napoleon Bonaparte** to come to power in 1799, first as a dictator, then as emperor. While the French Revolution threw off the power of a corrupt monarchy, its immediate results were likely not what the original perpetrators of the revolt had intended.

**Review Video: The French Revolution: Napoleon Bonaparte**
Visit mometrix.com/academy and enter code: 876330

## Industrial Revolution

### *Effects of the Industrial Revolution on Society*

The Industrial Revolution began in Great Britain in the 18th century, bringing coal- and steam-powered machinery into widespread use. Industry began a period of rapid growth with these developments. Goods that had previously been produced in small workshops or even in homes were produced more efficiently and in much larger quantities in **factories**. Where society had been largely agrarian-based, the focus swiftly shifted to an **industrial** outlook. As electricity and internal combustion engines replaced coal and steam as energy sources, even more drastic and rapid changes occurred. Western European countries, in particular, turned to colonialism, taking control of portions of Africa and Asia to ensure access to the raw materials needed to produce factory goods. Specialized labor became very much in demand, and businesses grew rapidly, creating monopolies, increasing world trade, and developing large urban centers. Even agriculture changed fundamentally as the Industrial Revolution led to a second **Agricultural Revolution** with the addition of new technology to advance agricultural production.

**Review Video: Industrialization**
Visit mometrix.com/academy and enter code: 893924

### *First and Second Phases of the Industrial Revolution*

The **first phase** of the Industrial Revolution took place from roughly 1750 to 1830. The textile industry experienced major changes as more and more elements of the process became mechanized. Mining benefited from the steam engine. Transportation became easier and more widely available as waterways were improved and the railroad came into prominence. In the **second phase**, from 1830 to 1910, industries further improved in efficiency, and new industries were introduced as photography, various chemical processes, and electricity became more widely available to produce new goods or new, improved versions of old goods. Petroleum and hydroelectricity became major sources of power. During this time, the Industrial Revolution spread out of Western Europe and into the US and Japan.

### *Political, Social and Economic Side Effects of the Industrial Revolution*

The Industrial Revolution led to widespread education, a wider franchise, and the development of mass communication in the political arena. **Economically**, conflicts arose between companies and their employees, as struggles for fair treatment and fair wages increased. Unions gained power and became more active. Government regulation over industries increased, but at the same time, growing businesses fought for the right to free enterprise. In the **social** sphere, populations increased and began to concentrate around centers of industry. Cities became larger and more densely populated. Scientific advancements led to more efficient agriculture, greater supply of goods, and increased knowledge of medicine and sanitation, leading to better overall health.

**Review Video: The Industrial Revolution**
Visit mometrix.com/academy and enter code: 372796

## Causes and Progression of the Russian Revolution of 1905

In Russia, rule lay in the hands of the **czars**, and the overall structure was **feudalistic**. Beneath the czars was a group of rich nobles, landowners whose lands were worked by peasants and serfs. The **Russo-Japanese War** (1904-1905) made conditions much worse for the lower classes. When peasants demonstrated outside the czar's Winter Palace, the palace guard fired upon the crowd. The demonstration had been organized by a trade union leader, and after the violent response, many unions and political parties blossomed and began to lead numerous strikes. When the economy ground to a halt, Czar Nicholas II signed a document known as the **October Manifesto**, which established a constitutional monarchy and gave legislative power to parliament. However, he violated the manifesto shortly thereafter, disbanding parliament and ignoring the civil liberties granted by the manifesto. This eventually led to the **Bolshevik Revolution**.

# World History 1914 to Present

## Nationalism and Its Effect on Society Through the 18th and 19th Centuries

Nationalism, put simply, is a strong belief in, identification with, and allegiance to a particular nation and people. **Nationalistic belief** unified various areas that had previously seen themselves as fragmented, which led to **patriotism** and, in some cases, **imperialism**. As nationalism grew, individual nations sought to grow, bringing in other, smaller states that shared similar characteristics such as language and cultural beliefs. Unfortunately, a major side effect of these growing nationalistic beliefs was often conflict and outright **war**.

In Europe, imperialism led countries to spread their influence into Africa and Asia. **Africa** was eventually divided among several European countries that wanted certain raw materials. **Asia** also came under European control, with the exception of China, Japan, and Siam (now Thailand). In the US, **Manifest Destiny** became the rallying cry as the country expanded west. Italy and Germany formed larger nations from a variety of smaller states.

**Review Video: Historical Nationalism**
Visit mometrix.com/academy and enter code: 510185

**Review Video: What is Nationalism?**
Visit mometrix.com/academy and enter code: 865693

## Events of World War I in the European Theater

WWI began in 1914 with the assassination of **Archduke Franz Ferdinand**, heir to the throne of Austria-Hungary, by a Serbian national. This led to a conflict between Austria-Hungary and Serbia that quickly escalated into the First World War. Europe split into the **Allies**—Britain, France, and Russia, and later Italy, Japan, and the US, against the **Central Powers**—Austria-Hungary, Germany, the Ottoman Empire, and Bulgaria. As the war spread, countries beyond Europe became involved. The war left Europe deeply in debt, and particularly devastated the German economy. The ensuing **Great Depression** made matters worse, and economic devastation opened the door for communist, fascist, and socialist governments to gain power.

## Trench Warfare and Its Use in World War I

Fighting during WWI largely took place in a series of **trenches** built along the Eastern and Western Fronts. These trenches added up to more than 24,000 miles. This produced fronts that stretched over 400 miles, from the coast of Belgium to the border of Switzerland. The Allies made use of straightforward open-air trenches with a front line, supporting lines, and communications lines. By contrast, the German trenches sometimes included well-equipped underground living quarters.

## Bolshevik Revolution

### *Factors Leading to the Bolshevik Revolution of 1917*

Throughout its modern history, Russia had lagged behind other countries in development. The continued existence of a feudal system, combined with harsh conditions and the overall size of the country, led to massive food shortages and increasingly harsh conditions for the majority of the population. The tyrannical rule of the czars only made this worse, as did repeated losses in various military conflicts. Increasing poverty, decreasing supplies, and the czar's violation of the **October Manifesto,** which had given some political power and civil rights to the people, finally came to a head with the **Bolshevik Revolution**.

### *Events of the Bolshevik Revolution*

A **workers' strike in Petrograd** in 1917 set the revolutionary wheels in motion when the army sided with the workers. While parliament set up a provisional government made up of nobles, the workers and military joined to form their own governmental system known as **soviets**, which consisted of local councils elected by the people. The ensuing chaos opened the doors for formerly exiled leaders Vladimir Lenin, Joseph Stalin, and Leon Trotsky to move in and gain popular support as well as the support of the Red Guard. Overthrowing parliament, they took power, creating a **communist** state in Russia. This development led to the spread of communism throughout Eastern Europe and elsewhere, greatly affecting diplomatic policies throughout the world for several decades.

## Communism vs. Socialism

At their roots, socialism and communism both focus on public ownership and distribution of goods and services. However, **communism** works toward revolution by drawing on what it sees to be inevitable class antagonism, eventually overthrowing the upper classes and the systems of capitalism. **Socialism** makes use of democratic procedures, building on the existing order. This was particularly true of the utopian socialists, who saw industrial capitalism as oppressive, not allowing workers to prosper. While socialism struggled between the World Wars, communism took hold, especially in Eastern Europe. After WWII, **democratic socialism** became more common. Later, **capitalism** took a stronger hold again, and today most industrialized countries in the western world function under an economy that mixes elements of capitalism and socialism.

**Review Video: Socialism**
Visit mometrix.com/academy and enter code: 917677

## Conditions that Led to the Rise of the Nazi Party in Germany

The **Great Depression** had a particularly devastating effect on Germany's economy, especially after the US was no longer able to supply reconstruction loans to help the country regain its footing. With unemployment rising rapidly, dissatisfaction with the government grew. Fascist and Communist parties rose, promising change and improvement.

Led by **Adolf Hitler**, the fascist **Nazi Party** eventually gained power in Parliament based on these promises and the votes of desperate German workers. When Hitler became chancellor, he launched numerous expansionist policies, violating the peace treaties that had ended WWI. His military buildup and conquering of neighboring countries sparked the aggression that soon led to WWII.

## Importance of the German Blitzkrieg to the Progression of World War II

The blitzkrieg, or "lightning war," consisted of fast, powerful surprise attacks that disrupted communications, made it difficult if not impossible for the victims to retaliate, and demoralized Germany's foes. The "blitz," or the aerial bombing of England in 1940, was one example, with bombings occurring in London and other cities 57 nights in a row. The **Battle of Britain** in 1940 also brought intense raids by Germany's air force, the **Luftwaffe**, mostly targeting ports and British air force bases. Eventually, Britain's Royal Air Force blocked the Luftwaffe, ending Germany's hopes for conquering Britain.

## Battle of the Bulge

Following the **D-Day Invasion**, Allied forces gained considerable ground and began a major campaign to push through Europe. In December of 1944, Hitler launched a counteroffensive, attempting to retake Antwerp, an important port. The ensuing battle became the largest land battle on the war's Western Front and was known as the Battle of the Ardennes, or the **Battle of the**

**Bulge**. The battle lasted from December 16, 1944, to January 25, 1945. The Germans pushed forward, making inroads into Allied lines, but in the end, the Allies brought the advance to a halt. The Germans were pushed back, with massive losses on both sides. However, those losses proved crippling to the German army.

## Holocaust

As Germany sank deeper and deeper into dire economic straits, the tendency was to look for a person or group of people to blame for the problems of the country. With distrust of the Jewish people already ingrained, it was easy for German authorities to set up the **Jews** as scapegoats for Germany's problems. Under the rule of Hitler and the Nazi party, the "Final Solution" for the supposed Jewish problem was devised. Millions of Jews, as well as Gypsies, homosexuals, communists, Catholics, the mentally ill, and others, simply named as criminals, were transported to concentration camps during the course of the war. At least six million were slaughtered in death camps such as **Auschwitz**, where horrible conditions and torture of prisoners were commonplace. The Allies were aware of rumors of mass slaughter throughout the war, but many discounted the reports. Only when troops went in to liberate the prisoners was the true horror of the concentration camps brought to light. The **Holocaust** resulted in massive loss of human life, but also in the loss and destruction of cultures. Because the genocide focused on specific ethnic groups, many traditions, histories, knowledge, and other cultural elements were lost, particularly among the Jewish and Gypsy populations. After World War II, the United Nations recognized **genocide** as a "crime against humanity." The UN passed the **Universal Declaration of Human Rights** in 1948 in order to further specify what rights the organization protected. Nazi war criminals faced justice during the **Nuremberg Trials**. There, individuals, rather than their governments, were held accountable for war crimes.

**Review Video: The Holocaust**
Visit mometrix.com/academy and enter code: 350695

## World War II and the Ensuing Diplomatic Climate that Led to the Cold War

With millions of military and civilian deaths and over 12 million persons displaced, **WWII** left large regions of Europe and Asia in disarray. **Communist** governments moved in with promises of renewed prosperity and economic stability. The **Soviet Union** backed communist regimes in much of Eastern Europe. In China, **Mao Zedong** led communist forces in the overthrow of the Chinese Nationalist Party and instituted a communist government in 1949. While the new communist governments restored a measure of stability to much of Eastern Europe, it brought its own problems, with dictatorial governments and an oppressive police force. The spread of communism also led to several years of tension between communist countries and the democratic West, as the West fought to slow the spread of oppressive regimes throughout the world. With both sides in possession of nuclear weapons, tensions rose. Each side feared the other would resort to nuclear attack. This standoff lasted until 1989, when the **Berlin Wall** fell. The Soviet Union was dissolved two years later.

## Origins of the United Nations

The United Nations (**UN**) came into being toward the end of World War II. A successor to the less-than-successful League of Nations formed after World War I, the UN built and improved on those ideas. Since its inception, the UN has worked to bring the countries of the world together for **diplomatic solutions** to international problems, including sanctions and other restrictions. It has also initiated military action, calling for peacekeeping troops from member countries to move against countries violating UN policies. The **Korean War** was the first example of UN involvement in an international conflict.

## EFFECTS OF DECOLONIZATION ON THE POST-WAR PERIOD

A rise of nationalism among European colonies led to many of them declaring independence. **India** and **Pakistan** became independent of Britain in 1947, and numerous African and Asian colonies declared independence as well. This period of **decolonization** lasted into the 1960s. Some colonies moved successfully into independence, but many, especially in Africa and Asia, struggled to create stable governments and economies and suffered from ethnic and religious conflicts, some of which continue today.

## FACTORS AND SHIFTS IN POWER THAT LED TO THE KOREAN WAR

In 1910, Japan annexed Korea and maintained this control until 1945. After WWII, Soviet and US troops occupied Korea, with the **Soviet Union** controlling North Korea and the **US** controlling South Korea. In 1947, the UN ordered elections in Korea to unify the country, but the Soviet Union refused to allow them to take place in North Korea, instead setting up a communist government. In 1950, the US withdrew troops, and the North Korean troops moved to invade South Korea. The **Korean War** was the first war in which the UN—or any international organization—played a major role. The US, Australia, Canada, France, Netherlands, Great Britain, Turkey, China, the USSR, and other countries sent troops at various times, for both sides, throughout the war. In 1953, the war ended in a truce, but no peace agreement was ever achieved, and Korea remains divided.

## EVENTS THAT LED TO THE VIETNAM WAR

Vietnam had previously been part of a French colony called French Indochina. The **Vietnam War** began with the **First Indochina War** from 1946 to 1954, in which France battled with the Democratic Republic of Vietnam, ruled by Ho Chi Minh.

In 1954, a siege at Dien Bien Phu ended in a Vietnamese victory. Vietnam was then divided into North and South, much like Korea. Communist forces controlled the North, and the South was controlled by South Vietnamese forces, supported by the US. Conflict ensued, leading to another war. US troops eventually led the fight, in support of South Vietnam. The war became a major political issue in the US, with many citizens protesting American involvement. In 1975, South Vietnam surrendered, and Vietnam became the **Socialist Republic of Vietnam**.

## GLOBALISM

In the modern era, globalism has emerged as a popular political ideology. **Globalism** is based on the idea that all people and all nations are **interdependent**. Each nation is dependent on one or more other nations for production of and markets for goods, and for income generation. Today's ease of international travel and communication, including technological advances such as the airplane, has heightened this sense of interdependence. The global economy and the general idea of globalism have shaped many economic and political choices since the beginning of the 20th century. Many of today's issues, including environmental awareness, economic struggles, and continued warfare, often require the cooperation of many countries if they are to be dealt with effectively.

## EFFECT OF GLOBALIZATION ON THE WAY COUNTRIES INTERACT WITH EACH OTHER

Countries worldwide often seek the same resources, leading to high demand, particularly for **nonrenewable resources**. This can result in heavy fluctuations in price. One major example is the demand for petroleum products such as oil and natural gas. Increased travel and communication make it possible to deal with diseases in remote locations; however, this also allows diseases to be spread via travelers.

A major factor contributing to increased globalization over the past few decades has been the **internet**. By allowing instantaneous communication with anyone nearly anywhere on the globe, the internet has led to interaction between far-flung individuals and countries, and an ever-increasing awareness of events all over the world.

**Review Video: Globalization**
Visit mometrix.com/academy and enter code: 551962

## Role of the Middle East in International Relations and Economics

The location on the globe, with ease of access to Europe and Asia, and its preponderance of oil deposits, makes the **Middle Eastern countries** crucial in many international issues, both diplomatic and economic. Because of its central location, the Middle East has been a hotbed for violence since before the beginning of recorded history. Conflicts over land, resources, and religious and political power continue in the area today, spurred by conflict over control of the area's vast oil fields as well as over territories that have been disputed for thousands of years.

## Major Occurrences of Genocide in Modern History

Five major occurrences of genocide in modern history other than the Holocaust are:

- **Armenian genocide**—from 1914 to 1918, the Young Turks, heirs to the Ottoman Empire, slaughtered between 800,000 and 1.5 million Armenians. This constituted approximately half of the Armenian population at the time.
- **Holodomor**—from 1932 to 1933, the people of Ukraine suffered the effects of a famine created by Joseph Stalin's collectivization of agriculture. Millions of Ukranians starved to death due to a lack of access to food.
- **Cambodian genocide**—from 1975 to 1979, the Khmer Rouge, a communist group, inflicted violence on the people of Cambodia. Between 1.5 million and 3 million Cambodians were killed. The Khmer Rouge were removed from power when the Vietnamese military took the capital of Cambodia.
- **Rwandan genocide**—in 1994, hundreds of thousands of Tutsis and Hutu sympathizers were slaughtered during the Rwandan Civil War. The UN did not act or authorize intervention during these atrocities.
- **Darfur genocide**—In 2003, militias tasked with combating rebel activity in Darfur kept the people of Darfur from accessing food and resources. This resulted in the death of hundreds of thousands of people in Darfur.

# United States History

## American History Pre-Columbian to 1789

### Well-Known Native Americans

The following are five well-known Native Americans and their roles in early US history:

1. **Squanto**, an Algonquian, helped early English settlers survive the hard winter by teaching them the native methods of planting corn, squash, and pumpkins.
2. **Pocahontas**, also Algonquian, became famous as a liaison with John Smith's Jamestown colony in 1607.
3. **Sacagawea**, a Shoshone, served a vital role in the Lewis and Clark expedition when the two explorers hired her as their guide in 1805.
4. **Crazy Horse** and **Sitting Bull** led Sioux and Cheyenne troops in the Battle of the Little Bighorn in 1876, soundly defeating George Armstrong Custer.
5. **Chief Joseph**, a leader of the Nez Perce who supported peaceful interaction with white settlers, attempted to relocate his tribe to Canada rather than move them to a reservation.

### Major Regional Native American Groups

The major regional Native American groups and the major traits of each are as follows:

- The **Algonquians** in the eastern part of the United States lived in wigwams. The northern tribes subsisted on hunting and gathering, while those who were farther south grew crops such as corn.
- The **Iroquois**, also an east coast tribe, spoke a different language from the Algonquians and lived in rectangular longhouses.
- The **Plains tribes** lived between the Mississippi River and the Rocky Mountains. These nomadic tribes lived in teepees and followed the buffalo herds. Plains tribes included the Sioux, Cheyenne, Comanche, and Blackfoot.
- **Pueblo tribes** included the Zuni, Hopi, and Acoma. They lived in the Southwest deserts in homes made of stone or adobe. They domesticated animals and cultivated corn and beans.
- On the Pacific coast, tribes such as the **Tlingit**, **Chinook**, and **Salish** lived on fish,deer, native berries, and roots. Their rectangular homes housed large family groups, and they used totem poles.
- In the far north, the **Aleuts** and **Inuit** lived in skin tents or igloos. Talented fishermen, they built kayaks and umiaks and also hunted caribou, seals, whales, and walrus.

**Review Video: Major Regional Native American Groups**
Visit mometrix.com/academy and enter code: 550136

### Age of Exploration

The Age of Exploration is also called the **Age of Discovery**. It is generally considered to have begun in the early 15th century and continued into the 17th century. Major developments of the **Age of Exploration** included technological advances in navigation, mapmaking, and shipbuilding. These advances led to expanded European exploration of the rest of the world. Explorers set out from several European countries, including Portugal, Spain, France, and England, seeking new routes to

Asia. These efforts led to the discovery of new lands, as well as colonization in India, Asia, Africa, and North America.

**Review Video: Age of Exploration**
Visit mometrix.com/academy and enter code: 612972

### Impact of Technological Advances in Navigation and Seafaring Exploration

For long ocean journeys, it was important for sailors to be able to find their way home even when their vessels sailed far out to sea. A variety of navigational tools enabled them to launch ambitious journeys over long distances. The **compass** and **astrolabe** were particularly important advancements. Chinese navigators used the magnetic compass in approximately 200 BC, and knowledge of the astrolabe came to Europe from Arab navigators and traders who had refined designs developed by the ancient Greeks. The Portuguese developed a ship called a **caravel** in the 1400s that incorporated navigational advancements with the ability to make long sea journeys. Equipped with this advanced vessel, the Portuguese achieved a major goal of the Age of Exploration by discovering a **sea route** from Europe to Asia in 1498.

### Significance of Christopher Columbus's Voyage

In 1492, Columbus, a Genoan explorer, obtained financial backing from King Ferdinand and Queen Isabella of Spain to seek a sea route to Asia. He sought a trade route with the Asian Indies to the west. With three ships, the *Niña*, the *Pinta*, and the *Santa Maria*, he eventually landed in the **West Indies**. While Columbus failed in his effort to discover a western route to Asia, he is credited with the discovery of the **Americas**.

**Review Video: Christopher Columbus**
Visit mometrix.com/academy and enter code: 496598

### French, Spanish, Dutch, and British Goals in Colonization of the Americas

France, Spain, the Netherlands, and England each had specific goals in the colonization of the Americas:

- Initial **French colonies** were focused on expanding the fur trade. Later, French colonization led to the growth of plantations in Louisiana, which brought numerous African slaves to the New World.
- **Spanish colonists** came to look for wealth and to convert the natives to Christianity. For some, the desire for gold led to mining in the New World, while others established large ranches.
- The **Dutch** were also involved in the fur trade and imported slaves as the need for laborers increased.
- **British colonists** arrived with various goals. Some were simply looking for additional income, while others were fleeing Britain to escape religious persecution.

**Review Video: Colonization of the Americas**
Visit mometrix.com/academy and enter code: 438412

### New England Colonies

The New England colonies were New Hampshire, Connecticut, Rhode Island and Massachusetts. These colonies were founded largely to escape **religious persecution** in England. The beliefs of the **Puritans**, who migrated to America in the 1600s, significantly influenced the development of these colonies. Situated in the northeast coastal areas of America, the New England colonies featured numerous harbors as well as dense forests. The soil, however, was rocky and had a very short growing season, so was not well suited for agriculture. The economy of New England during the colonial period centered around fishing, shipbuilding and trade along with some small farms and lumber mills. Although some groups congregated in small farms, life centered mainly in towns and cities where **merchants** largely controlled the trade economy. Coastal cities such as Boston grew and thrived.

**Review Video: The Massachusetts Bay Colony**
Visit mometrix.com/academy and enter code: 407058

## Middle or Middle Atlantic Colonies

The Middle or Middle Atlantic Colonies were New York, New Jersey, Pennsylvania, and Delaware. Unlike the New England colonies, where most colonists were from England and Scotland, the Middle Colonies founders were from various countries, including the Netherlands and Sweden. Various factors led these colonists to America. More fertile than New England, the Middle Colonies became major producers of **crops**, including rye, oats, potatoes, wheat, and barley. Some particularly wealthy inhabitants owned large farms and/or businesses. Farmers, in general, were able to produce enough to have a surplus to sell. Tenant farmers also rented land from larger landowners.

## Southern Colonies

The Southern Colonies were Maryland, Virginia, North Carolina, South Carolina, and Georgia. Of the Southern Colonies, Virginia was the first permanent English colony and Georgia the last. The warm climate and rich soil of the south encouraged **agriculture**, and the growing season was long. As a result, economy in the south was based largely on labor-intensive **plantations**. Crops included tobacco, rice, and indigo, all of which became valuable cash crops. Most land in the south was controlled by wealthy plantation owners and farmers. Labor on the farms came in the form of indentured servants and African slaves. The first of these **African slaves** arrived in Virginia in 1619.

**Review Video: Southern Colonies: An Overview**
Visit mometrix.com/academy and enter code: 703830

**Review Video: The English Colony of Virginia**
Visit mometrix.com/academy and enter code: 537399

## Significance of the French and Indian Wars

The **British defeat of the Spanish Armada** in 1588 led to the decline of Spanish power in Europe. This, in turn, led the British and French into battle several times between 1689 and 1748. These wars were:

- King William's War, or the Nine Years War, 1689-1697. This war was fought largely in Flanders.
- The War of Spanish Succession, or Queen Anne's War, 1702-1713
- War of Austrian Succession, or King George's War, 1740-1748

The fourth and final war, the **French and Indian War** (1754-1763), was fought largely in the North American territory and resulted in the end of France's reign as a colonial power in North America. Although the French held many advantages, including more cooperative colonists and numerous Native American allies, the strong leadership of **William Pitt** eventually led the British to victory.

Costs incurred during the wars eventually led to discontent in the colonies and helped spark the **American Revolution**.

**Review Video: French and Indian War**
Visit mometrix.com/academy and enter code: 502183

## Navigation Acts

The Navigation Acts, enacted in 1651, were an attempt by Britain to dominate international trade. Aimed largely at the Dutch, the acts banned foreign ships from transporting goods to the British colonies and from transporting goods to Britain from elsewhere in Europe. While the restrictions on trade angered some colonists, these acts were helpful to other American colonists who, as members of the British Empire, were legally able to provide ships for Britain's growing trade interests and use the ships for their own trading ventures. By the time the French and Indian War had ended, one-third of British merchant ships were built in the American colonies. Many colonists amassed fortunes in the shipbuilding trade.

## Acts of British Parliament that Occurred After the French and Indian Wars

After the French and Indian Wars, the British Parliament passed four major acts:

1. The **Sugar Act**, 1764—this act not only required taxes to be collected on molasses brought into the colonies but gave British officials the right to search the homes of anyone suspected of violating it.
2. The **Stamp Act**, 1765—this act taxed printed materials such as newspapers and legal documents. Protests led the Stamp Act to be repealed in 1766, but the repeal also included the Declaratory Act, which stated that Parliament had the right to govern the colonies.
3. The **Quartering Act**, 1765—this act required colonists to provide accommodations and supplies for British troops. In addition, colonists were prohibited from settling west of the Appalachians until given permission by Britain.
4. The **Townshend Acts**, 1767—these acts taxed paper, paint, lead, and tea that came into the colonies. Colonists led boycotts in protest, and in Massachusetts leaders like Samuel and John Adams began to organize resistance against British rule.

## Britain's Taxation of the American Colonies After the French and Indian War

The French and Indian War created circumstances for which the British desperately needed more revenue. These needs included:

- Paying off the war debt
- Defending the expanding empire
- Governing Britain's 33 far-flung colonies, including the American colonies

To meet these needs, the British passed additional laws, increasing revenues from the colonies. Because they had spent so much money to defend the American colonies, the British felt it was appropriate to collect considerably higher **taxes** from them. The colonists felt this was unfair, and many were led to protest the increasing taxes. Eventually, protest led to violence.

## Triangular Trade

Triangular trade began in the colonies with ships setting off for **Africa**, carrying rum. In Africa, the rum was traded for gold or slaves. Ships then went from Africa to the **West Indies**, trading slaves for sugar, molasses, or money. To complete the triangle, the ships returned to the **colonies** with sugar or molasses to make more rum, as well as stores of gold and silver. This trade triangle violated the Molasses Act of 1733, which required the colonists to pay high duties to Britain on molasses acquired from French, Dutch, and Spanish colonies. The colonists ignored these duties, and the British government adopted a policy of salutary neglect by not enforcing them.

**Review Video: What was the Triangular Trade?**
Visit mometrix.com/academy and enter code: 415470

## Effects of New Laws on British-Colonial Relations

While earlier revenue-generating acts such as the Navigation Acts brought money to the colonists, the new laws after 1763 required colonists to pay money back to **Britain**. The British felt this was fair since the colonists were British subjects and since they had incurred debt protecting the Colonies. The colonists felt it was not only unfair but illegal.

The development of **local government** in America had given the colonists a different view of the structure and role of government. This made it difficult for the British to understand the colonists' protests against what the British felt was a fair and reasonable solution to the mother country's financial problems.

## Factors that Led to Increasing Discontent in the American Colonies

More and more colonists were born on American soil, decreasing any sense of kinship with the far-away British rulers. Their new environment had led to new ideas of government and a strong view of the colonies as a separate entity from Britain. Colonists were allowed to **self-govern** in domestic issues, but **Britain** controlled international issues. In fact, the American colonies were largely left to form their own local government bodies, giving them more freedom than any other colonial territory. This gave the colonists a sense of **independence**, which led them to resent control from Britain. Threats during the French and Indian War led the colonists to call for unification in order to protect themselves.

## Colonial Government and British Government Differences that Led to "No Taxation Without Representation"

As new towns and other legislative districts developed in America, the colonists began to practice **representative government**. Colonial legislative bodies were made up of elected representatives chosen by male property owners in the districts. These individuals represented the interests of the districts from which they had been elected.

By contrast, in Britain, the **Parliament** represented the entire country. Parliament was not elected to represent individual districts. Instead, they represented specific classes. Because of this drastically different approach to government, the British did not understand the colonists' statement that they had no representation in the British Parliament.

## Factors that Led to the Boston Massacre

With the passage of the **Stamp Act**, nine colonies met in New York to demand its repeal. Elsewhere, protest arose in New York City, Philadelphia, Boston, and other cities. These protests sometimes escalated into violence, often targeting ruling British officials. The passage of the **Townshend Acts** in 1767 led to additional tension in the colonies. The British sent troops to New York City and Boston. On March 5, 1770, protesters began to taunt the British troops, throwing snowballs. The soldiers responded by firing into the crowd. This clash between protesters and soldiers led to five deaths and eight injuries, and was christened the **Boston Massacre**. Shortly thereafter, Britain repealed the majority of the Townshend Acts.

## Tea Act that Led to the Boston Tea Party

The majority of the **Townshend Acts** were repealed after the Boston Massacre in 1770, but Britain kept the tax on tea. In 1773, the **Tea Act** was passed. This allowed the East India Company to sell tea for much lower prices and also allowed them to bypass American distributors, selling directly to shopkeepers instead. Colonial tea merchants saw this as a direct assault on their business. In December of 1773, the **Sons of Liberty** boarded ships in Boston Harbor and dumped 342 chests of tea into the sea in protest of the new laws. This act of protest came to be known as the **Boston Tea Party**.

## Coercive Acts Passed after the Boston Tea Party

The Coercive Acts passed by Britain in 1774 were meant to punish Massachusetts for defying British authority. The following were also known as the **Intolerable Acts**:

- Shut down ports in Boston until the city paid back the value of the tea destroyed during the Boston Tea Party
- Required that local government officials in Massachusetts be appointed by the governor rather than being elected by the people
- Allowed trials of British soldiers to be transferred to Britain rather than being held in Massachusetts
- Required locals to provide lodging for British soldiers any time there was a disturbance, even if lodging required them to stay in private homes

These acts led to the assembly of the First Continental Congress in Philadelphia on September 5, 1774. Fifty-five delegates met, representing 12 of the American colonies. They sought compromise with England over England's increasingly harsh efforts to control the colonies.

## First Continental Congress

The goal of the First Continental Congress was to achieve a peaceful agreement with Britain. Made up of delegates from 12 of the 13 colonies, the Congress affirmed loyalty to Britain and the power of Parliament to dictate foreign affairs in the colonies. However, they demanded that the **Intolerable Acts** be repealed, and instituted a trade embargo with Britain until this came to pass.

In response, George III of England declared that the American colonies must submit or face military action. The British sought to end assemblies that opposed their policies. These assemblies gathered weapons and began to form militias. On April 19, 1775, the British military was ordered to disperse a meeting of the Massachusetts Assembly. A battle ensued on Lexington Common as the armed colonists resisted. The resulting battles became the **Battle of Lexington and Concord**—the first battles of the **American Revolution**.

## Significance of the Second Continental Congress

The Second Continental Congress met in Philadelphia on May 10, 1775, a month after Lexington and Concord. Their discussions centered on the defense of the American colonies and how to conduct the growing war, as well as local government. The delegates also discussed declaring independence from Britain, with many members in favor of this drastic move. They established an army, and on June 15, named **George Washington** as its commander in chief. By 1776, it was obvious that there was no turning back from full-scale war with Britain. The colonial delegates of the Continental Congress signed the **Declaration of Independence** on July 4, 1776.

**Review Video: The First and Second Continental Congress**
Visit mometrix.com/academy and enter code: 835211

## Origins and Basic Ideas of the Declaration of Independence

Penned by Thomas Jefferson and signed on July 4, 1776, the **Declaration of Independence** stated that King George III had violated the rights of the colonists and was establishing a tyrannical reign over them. Many of Jefferson's ideas of natural rights and property rights were shaped by 17th-century philosopher **John Locke**. Jefferson asserted all people's rights to "life, liberty and the pursuit of happiness." Locke's comparable idea asserted "life, liberty, and private property." Both felt that the purpose of government was to protect the rights of the people, and that individual rights were more important than individuals' obligations to the state.

**Review Video: Declaration of Independence**
Visit mometrix.com/academy and enter code: 256838

## Battles of the Revolutionary War

The following are five major battles of the Revolutionary War and their significance:

- The **Battle of Lexington and Concord** (April 1775) is considered the first engagement of the Revolutionary War.
- The **Battle of Bunker Hill** (June 1775) was one of the bloodiest of the entire war. Although American troops withdrew, about half of the British army was lost. The colonists proved they could stand against professional British soldiers. In August, Britain declared that the American colonies were officially in a state of rebellion.
- The first colonial victory occurred in Trenton, New Jersey, when Washington and his troops **crossed the Delaware River** on Christmas Day, 1776, for a December 26 surprise attack on British and Hessian troops.
- The **Battle of Saratoga** effectively ended a plan to separate the New England colonies from their Southern counterparts. The surrender of British general John Burgoyne led to France joining the war as allies of the Americans and is generally considered a turning point of the war.
- On October 19, 1781, General Cornwallis surrendered after a defeat in the **Battle of Yorktown**, ending the Revolutionary War.

**Review Video: The American Revolutionary War**
Visit mometrix.com/academy and enter code: 935282

## Significance of the Treaty of Paris

The Treaty of Paris was signed on September 3, 1783, bringing an official end to the Revolutionary War. In this document, Britain officially recognized the United States of America as an **independent nation**. The treaty established the Mississippi River as the country's western border. The treaty also restored Florida to Spain, while France reclaimed African and Caribbean colonies seized by the British in 1763. On November 25, 1783, the last British troops departed from the newly born United States of America.

## Significance of the Articles of Confederation

A precursor to the Constitution, the **Articles of Confederation** represented the first attempt of the newly independent colonies to establish the basics of government. The Continental Congress approved the Articles on November 15, 1777. They went into effect on March 1, 1781, following ratification by the thirteen states. The articles prevented a central government from gaining too much power, instead giving power to a **congressional body** made up of **delegates** from all thirteen states. However, the individual states retained final authority.

Without a strong central **executive**, though, this weak alliance among the new states proved ineffective in settling disputes or enforcing laws. The idea of a weak central government needed to be revised. Recognition of these weaknesses eventually led to the drafting of a new document, the **Constitution**.

**Review Video: Articles of Confederation**
Visit mometrix.com/academy and enter code: 927401

## Initial Proposition and Draft of the Constitution

Delegates from twelve of the thirteen states (Rhode Island was not represented) met in Philadelphia in May of 1787, initially intending to revise the Articles of Confederation. However, it quickly became apparent that a simple revision would not provide the workable governmental structure the newly formed country needed. After vowing to keep all the proceedings secret until the final document was completed, the delegates set out to draft what would eventually become the **Constitution of the United States of America**. By keeping the negotiations secret, the delegates were able to present a completed document to the country for ratification, rather than having every small detail hammered out by the general public.

## General Structure of Government Proposed by the Delegates

The delegates agreed that the new nation required a **strong central government** but that its overall power should be **limited**. The various branches of the government should have **balanced power**, so that no one group could control the others. Final power belonged to the **citizens** who voted officials into office based on who would provide the best representation.

## Objections Against the Constitution

Once the Constitution was drafted, it was presented for approval by the states. Nine states needed to approve the document for it to become official. However, debate and discussion continued. Major **concerns** included:

- There was no bill of rights to protect individual freedoms.
- States felt too much power was being handed over to the central government.
- Voters wanted more control over their elected representatives.

Discussion about necessary changes to the Constitution was divided into two camps: Federalists and Anti-Federalists. **Federalists** wanted a strong central government. **Anti-Federalists** wanted to prevent a tyrannical government from developing if a central government held too much power

## Major Players in the Federalist and Anti-Federalist camps

Major Federalist leaders included Alexander Hamilton, John Jay, and James Madison. They wrote a series of letters, called the **Federalist Papers**, aimed at convincing the states to ratify the Constitution. These were published in New York papers. Anti-Federalists included Thomas Jefferson and Patrick Henry. They argued against the Constitution as it was originally drafted in a series of **Anti-Federalist Papers**.

The final compromise produced a strong central government controlled by checks and balances. A **Bill of Rights** was also added, becoming the first ten amendments to the Constitution. These amendments protected rights such as freedom of speech, freedom of religion, and other basic rights. Aside from various amendments added throughout the years, the United States Constitution has remained unchanged.

### Individuals Who Formed the First Administration of the New Government

The individuals who formed the first administration of the new government were:

- **George Washington**—elected as the first President of the United States in 1789
- **John Adams**—finished second in the election and became the first Vice President
- **Thomas Jefferson**—appointed by Washington as Secretary of State
- **Alexander Hamilton**—appointed Secretary of the Treasury

### Significance of the Virginia Plan, the New Jersey Plan, and the Great Compromise

Disagreement immediately occurred between delegates from large states and those from smaller states. James Madison and Edmund Randolph (the governor of Virginia) felt that representation in Congress should be based on state population. This was the **Virginia Plan**. The **New Jersey Plan**, presented by William Paterson from New Jersey, proposed that each state should have equal representation. Finally, Roger Sherman from Connecticut formulated the **Connecticut Compromise**, also called the Great Compromise. The result was the familiar structure we have today. Each state has the equal representation of two Senators in the Senate, with the number of representatives in the House of Representatives based on population. This is called a **bicameral congress**. Both houses may draft bills, but financial matters must originate in the House of Representatives.

### Effects of the Three-fifths Compromise and the Number of Representatives for Each State

During debate on the US Constitution, a disagreement arose between the Northern and Southern states involving how **slaves** should be counted when determining a state's quota of representatives. In the South, large numbers of slaves were commonly used to run plantations. Delegates wanted slaves to be counted to determine the number of representatives but not counted to determine the amount of taxes the states would pay. The Northern states wanted exactly the opposite arrangement. The final decision was to count three-fifths of the slave population both for tax purposes and to determine representation. This was called the **Three-fifths Compromise**.

### Provisions of the Commerce Compromise

The Commerce Compromise also resulted from a North/South disagreement. In the North, the economy was centered on **industry and trade**. The Southern economy was largely **agricultural**. The Northern states wanted to give the new government the ability to regulate exports as well as trade between the states. The South opposed this plan. Another compromise was in order. In the end, Congress received regulatory power over all trade, including the ability to collect **tariffs** on exported goods. In the South, this raised another red flag regarding the slave trade, as they were concerned about the effect on their economy if tariffs were levied on slaves. The final agreement allowed importing slaves to continue for twenty years without government intervention. Import taxes on slaves were limited, and after the year 1808, Congress could decide whether to allow continued imports of slaves.

## American History 1790 to 1898

### Alien and Sedition Acts

When **John Adams** became president, a war was raging between Britain and France. While Adams and the **Federalists** backed the British, Thomas Jefferson and the **Republican Party** supported the French. The United States nearly went to war with France during this time period, while France worked to spread its international standing and influence under the leadership of **Napoleon Bonaparte**. The **Alien and Sedition Acts** grew out of this conflict and made it illegal to speak in a hostile fashion against the existing government. They also allowed the president to deport anyone in the US who was not a citizen and who was suspected of treason or treasonous activity. When Jefferson became the third president in 1800, he repealed these four laws and pardoned anyone who had been convicted under them.

## Development of Political Parties in Early US Government

Many in the US were against political parties after seeing the way parties, or factions, functioned in Britain. The factions in Britain were more interested in personal profit than the overall good of the country, and they did not want this to happen in the US.

However, the differences of opinion between Thomas Jefferson and Alexander Hamilton led to the formation of **political parties**. Hamilton favored a stronger central government, while Jefferson felt that more power should remain with the states. Jefferson was in favor of strict Constitutional interpretation, while Hamilton believed in a more flexible approach. As others joined the two camps, Hamilton backers began to call themselves **Federalists**, while those supporting Jefferson became identified as **Democratic-Republicans**.

## Development of the Whig, the Democratic, and the Republican Parties

**Thomas Jefferson** was elected president in 1800 and again in 1804. The **Federalist Party** began to decline, and its major figure, Alexander Hamilton, died in a duel with Aaron Burr in 1804. By 1816, the Federalist Party had virtually disappeared.

New parties sprang up to take its place. After 1824, the **Democratic-Republican Party** suffered a split. The **Whigs** rose, backing John Quincy Adams and industrial growth. The new Democratic Party formed in opposition to the Whigs, and their candidate, Andrew Jackson, was elected as president in 1828.

By the 1850s, issues regarding slavery led to the formation of the **Republican Party**, which was anti-slavery, while the Democratic Party, with a larger interest in the South, favored slavery. This Republican/Democrat division formed the basis of today's **two-party system**.

## Significance of Marbury v. Madison

The main duty of the Supreme Court today is **judicial review**. This power was largely established by **Marbury v. Madison**. When John Adams was voted out of office in 1800, he worked during his final days in office to appoint Federalist judges to Supreme Court positions, knowing Jefferson, his replacement, held opposing views. As late as March 3, the day before Jefferson was to take office, Adams made last-minute appointments referred to as "Midnight Judges." One of the late appointments was William Marbury. The next day, March 4, Jefferson ordered his Secretary of State, James Madison, not to deliver Marbury's commission. This decision was backed by Chief Justice Marshall, who determined that the **Judiciary Act of 1789**, which granted the power to deliver commissions, was illegal in that it gave the Judicial Branch powers not granted in the Constitution. This case set precedent for the Supreme Court to nullify laws it found to be **unconstitutional**.

**Review Video: Marbury v Madison**
Visit mometrix.com/academy and enter code: 573964

## Political Motivations Behind France Selling the Louisiana Purchase

With tension still high between France and Britain, Napoleon was in need of money to support his continuing war efforts. To secure necessary funds, he decided to sell the **Louisiana Territory** to the US. President **Thomas Jefferson** wanted to buy New Orleans, feeling US trade was made vulnerable to both Spain and France at that port. Instead, Napoleon sold him the entire territory for the bargain price of $15 million. The Louisiana Territory was larger than all the rest of the United States put together, and it eventually became 15 additional states.

**Federalists** in Congress were opposed to the purchase. They feared that the Louisiana Purchase would extend slavery, and that further western growth would weaken the power of the northern states.

## Lewis and Clark Expedition

The purchase of the **Louisiana Territory** from France in 1803 more than doubled the size of the United States. President Thomas Jefferson wanted to have the area mapped and explored, since much of the territory was wilderness. He chose Meriwether Lewis and William Clark to head an expedition into the Louisiana Territory. After two years, Lewis and Clark returned, having traveled all the way to the Pacific Ocean. They brought maps, detailed journals, and a multitude of information about the wide expanse of land they had traversed. The **Lewis and Clark Expedition** opened up the west in the Louisiana Territory and beyond for further exploration and settlement.

**Review Video: Lewis and Clark Expedition**
Visit mometrix.com/academy and enter code: 570657

## Causes and Result of the War of 1812

The War of 1812 grew out of the continuing tension between France and Great Britain. Napoleon continued striving to conquer Britain, while the US continued trade with both countries but favored France and the French colonies. Because of what Britain saw as an alliance between America and France, they determined to bring an end to trade between the two nations.

With the British preventing US trade with the French and the French preventing trade with the British, James Madison's presidency introduced acts to **regulate international trade**. If either Britain or France removed their restrictions, America would not trade with the other country. Napoleon acted first, and Madison prohibited trade with England. England saw this as the US formally siding with the French, and war ensued in 1812.

The **War of 1812** has been called the **Second American Revolution**. It established the superiority of the US naval forces and reestablished US independence from Britain and Europe.

The British had two major objections to America's continued trade with France. First, they saw the US as helping France's war effort by providing supplies and goods. Second, the United States had grown into a competitor, taking trade and money away from British ships and tradesmen. In its attempts to end American trade with France, the British put into effect the **Orders in Council**, which made any and all French-owned ports off-limits to American ships. They also began to seize American ships and conscript their crews.

**Review Video: Overview of the War of 1812**
Visit mometrix.com/academy and enter code: 507716

**Review Video: Opinions About the War of 1812**
Visit mometrix.com/academy and enter code: 274558

## Major Military Events of the War of 1812

Two major naval battles, at **Lake Erie** and **Lake Champlain**, kept the British from invading the US via Canada. American attempts to conquer Canadian lands were not successful.

In another memorable British attack, the British invaded Washington, DC and burned the White House on August 24, 1814. Legend has it that **Dolley Madison**, the First Lady, salvaged the portrait of George Washington from the fire. On Christmas Eve, 1814, the **Treaty of Ghent** officially ended the war. However, Andrew Jackson, unaware that the war was over, managed another victory at New Orleans on January 8, 1815. This victory improved American morale and led to a new wave of national pride and support known as the "**Era of Good Feelings**."

## Influence of the American System on American Economics

Spurred by the trade conflicts of the War of 1812 and supported by Henry Clay among others, the **American System** set up tariffs to help protect American interests from competition with overseas products. Reducing competition led to growth in employment and an overall increase in American industry. The higher tariffs also provided funds for the government to pay for various improvements. Congress passed high tariffs in 1816 and also chartered a federal bank. The **Second Bank of the United States** was given the job of regulating America's money supply.

## McCulloch v. Maryland

Judicial review was further exercised by the Supreme Court in **McCulloch v. Maryland**. When Congress chartered a national bank, the **Second Bank of the United States**, Maryland voted to tax any bank business dealing with banks chartered outside the state, including the federally chartered bank. Andrew McCulloch, an employee of the Second Bank of the US in Baltimore, refused to pay this tax. The resulting lawsuit from the State of Maryland went to the Supreme Court for judgment.

John Marshall, Chief Justice of the Supreme Court, stated that Congress was within its rights to charter a national bank. In addition, the State of Maryland did not have the power to levy a tax on the federal bank or on the federal government in general. In cases where state and federal government collided, precedent was set for the **federal government** to prevail.

## Effects of the Missouri Compromise on the Tensions Between the North and South

By 1819, the United States had developed a tenuous balance between slave and free states, with exactly 22 senators in Congress from each faction. However, Missouri was ready to join the union. As a slave state, it would tip the balance in Congress. To prevent this imbalance, the **Missouri Compromise** brought the northern part of Massachusetts into the union as Maine, establishing it as a free state to balance the admission of Missouri as a slave state. In addition, the remaining portion of the Louisiana Purchase was to remain free north of **latitude 36°30'**. Since cotton did not grow well this far north, this limitation was acceptable to congressmen representing the slave states.

However, the proposed Missouri constitution presented a problem, as it outlawed immigration of free blacks into the state. Another compromise was in order, this time proposed by **Henry Clay**. According to this new compromise, Missouri would never pass a law that prevented anyone from entering the state. Through this and other work, Clay earned his title of the "**Great Compromiser**."

**Review Video: What was the Missouri Compromise?**
Visit mometrix.com/academy and enter code: 848091

## Monroe Doctrine

On December 2, 1823, President Monroe delivered a message to Congress in which he introduced the **Monroe Doctrine**. In this address, he stated that any attempts by European powers to establish new colonies on the North American continent would be considered interference in American politics. The US would stay out of European matters, and expected Europe to offer America the same courtesy. This approach to foreign policy stated in no uncertain terms that America would not tolerate any new European colonies in the New World, and that events occurring in Europe would no longer influence the policies and doctrines of the US.

## Effect of the Treaty of Paris on Native Americans

After the Revolutionary War, the **Treaty of Paris**, which outlined the terms of surrender of the British to the Americans, granted large parcels of land to the US that were occupied by Native Americans. The new government attempted to claim the land, treating the natives as a conquered people. This approach proved unenforceable.

Next, the government tried purchasing the land from the Native Americans via a series of **treaties** as the country expanded westward. In practice, however, these treaties were not honored, and Native Americans were simply dislocated and forced to move farther and farther west, often with military action, as American expansion continued.

## Indian Removal Act of 1830 and the Treaty of New Echota

The Indian Removal Act of 1830 gave the new American government power to form treaties with Native Americans. In theory, America would claim land east of the Mississippi in exchange for land west of the Mississippi, to which the natives would relocate voluntarily. In practice, many tribal leaders were forced into signing the treaties, and relocation at times occurred by force.

The **Treaty of New Echota** in 1835 was supposedly a treaty between the US government and Cherokee tribes in Georgia. However, the treaty was not signed by tribal leaders but rather by a small portion of the represented people. The leaders protested and refused to leave, but President Martin Van Buren enforced the treaty by sending soldiers. During their forced relocation, more than 4,000 Cherokees died on what became known as the **Trail of Tears**.

**Review Video: Indian Removal Act**
Visit mometrix.com/academy and enter code: 666738

## Jacksonian Democracy vs. Preceding Political Climate

Jacksonian Democracy is largely seen as a shift from politics favoring the wealthy to politics favoring the common man. The right to vote was given to all free white males, not just property owners, as had been the case previously. Jackson's approach favored the patronage system, laissez-faire economics, and relocation of the Native American tribes from the Southeast portion of the country. Jackson opposed the formation of a federal bank and allowed the Second Bank of the United States to collapse by vetoing a bill to renew the charter. Jackson also faced the challenge of the **Nullification Crisis** when South Carolina claimed that it could ignore or nullify any federal law it considered unconstitutional. Jackson sent troops to the state to enforce the protested tariff laws, and a compromise engineered by Henry Clay in 1833 settled the matter for the time being.

### SECOND GREAT AWAKENING

Led by Protestant evangelical leaders, the **Second Great Awakening** occurred between 1800 and 1830. Several missionary groups grew out of the movement, including the **American Home Missionary Society**, which formed in 1826. The ideas behind the Second Great Awakening focused on personal responsibility, both as an individual and in response to injustice and suffering. The **American Bible Society** and the **American Tract Society** provided literature, while various traveling preachers spread the word. New denominations arose, including the Latter-day Saints and Seventh-day Adventists.

Another movement associated with the Second Great Awakening was the **temperance movement**, focused on ending the production and use of alcohol. One major organization behind the temperance movement was the **Society for the Promotion of Temperance**, formed in 1826 in Boston.

### ATTITUDES TOWARD EDUCATION IN THE EARLY 19TH CENTURY

**Horace Mann**, among others, felt that schools could help children become better citizens, keep them away from crime, prevent poverty, and help American society become more unified. His *Common School Journal* brought his ideas of the importance of education into the public consciousness and proposed his suggestions for an improved American education system. Increased literacy led to increased awareness of current events, Western expansion, and other major developments of the time period. Public interest and participation in the arts and literature also increased. By the end of the 19th century, all children had access to a **free public elementary education**.

### DEVELOPMENT OF ECONOMIC TRENDS AS THE US CONTINUED TO GROW

In the Northeast, the economy mostly depended on **manufacturing, industry, and industrial development**. This led to a dichotomy between rich business owners and industrial leaders and the much poorer workers who supported their businesses. The South continued to depend on **agriculture**, especially on large-scale farms or plantations worked mostly by slaves and indentured servants. In the West, where new settlements had begun to develop, the land was largely wild. Growing communities were essentially **agricultural**, raising crops and livestock. The differences between regions led each to support different interests both politically and economically.

### INDUSTRIAL ACTIVITY BEFORE AND AFTER 1800

During the 18th century, goods were often manufactured in houses or small shops. With increased technology allowing for the use of machines, **factories** began to develop. In factories, a large volume of salable goods could be produced in a much shorter amount of time. Many Americans, including increasing numbers of **immigrants**, found jobs in these factories, which were in constant need of labor. Another major invention was the **cotton gin**, which significantly decreased the processing time of cotton and was a major factor in the rapid expansion of cotton production in the South.

### DEVELOPMENT OF LABOR MOVEMENTS IN THE 1800S

In 1751, a group of bakers held a protest in which they stopped baking bread. This was technically the first American **labor strike**. In the 1830s and 1840s, labor movements began in earnest. Boston's masons, carpenters, and stoneworkers protested the length of the workday, fighting to reduce it to ten hours. In 1844, a group of women in the textile industry also fought to reduce their workday to ten hours, forming the **Lowell Female Labor Reform Association**. Many other protests occurred and organizations developed through this time period with the same goal in mind.

## Major Ideas Driving American Foreign Policy

The three major ideas driving American foreign policy during its early years were:

- **Isolationism**—the early US government did not intend to establish colonies, though they did plan to grow larger within the bounds of North America.
- **No entangling alliances**—both George Washington and Thomas Jefferson were opposed to forming any permanent alliances with other countries or becoming involved in other countries' internal issues.
- **Nationalism**—a positive patriotic feeling about the United States blossomed quickly among its citizens, particularly after the War of 1812, when the US once again defeated Britain. The Industrial Revolution also sparked increased nationalism by allowing even the most far-flung areas of the US to communicate with each other via telegraph and the expanding railroad.

## Effects of Manifest Destiny on American Politics

In the 1800s, many believed America was destined by God to expand west, bringing as much of the North American continent as possible under the umbrella of the US government. With the Northwest Ordinance and the Louisiana Purchase, over half of the continent became American. However, the rapid and relentless expansion brought conflict with the Native Americans, Great Britain, Mexico, and Spain. One result of "**Manifest Destiny**" was the **Mexican-American War** from 1846 to 1848. By the end of the war, Texas, California, and a large portion of what is now the American Southwest joined the growing nation. Conflict also arose over the **Oregon Territory**, shared by the US and Britain. In 1846, President James Polk resolved this problem by compromising with Britain, establishing a US boundary south of the 49th parallel.

**Review Video: What is the Manifest Destiny?**
Visit mometrix.com/academy and enter code: 957409

## Mexican-American War

Spain had held colonial interests in America since the 1540s—earlier even than Great Britain. In 1810, **Mexico** revolted against Spain, becoming a free nation in 1821. **Texas** followed suit, declaring its independence after an 1836 revolution. In 1844, the Democrats pressed President Tyler to annex Texas. Unlike his predecessor, Andrew Jackson, Tyler agreed to admit Texas into the Union, and in 1845, Texas became a state.

During Mexico's war for independence, the nation incurred $4.5 million in war debts to the US. Polk offered to forgive the debts in return for New Mexico and Upper California, but Mexico refused. In 1846, war was declared in response to a Mexican attack on American troops along the southern border of Texas. Additional conflict arose in Congress over the **Wilmot Proviso**, which stated that slavery was prohibited in any territory the US acquired from Mexico as a result of the **Mexican-American War**. The war ended in 1848.

**Review Video: When was the Mexican-American War?**
Visit mometrix.com/academy and enter code: 271216

**Review Video: Sectional Crisis: The Wilmot Proviso**
Visit mometrix.com/academy and enter code: 974842

## Popular Sovereignty and the Compromise of 1850

In addition to the pro-slavery and anti-slavery factions, a third group rose, who felt that each individual state should decide whether to allow or permit slavery within its borders. The idea that a state could make its own choices was referred to as **popular sovereignty**.

When California applied to join the union in 1849, the balance of congressional power was again threatened. The **Compromise of 1850** introduced a group of laws meant to bring an end to the conflict:

- California's admittance as a free state
- The outlaw of the slave trade in Washington, DC
- An increase in efforts to capture escaped slaves
- The right of New Mexico and Utah territories to decide individually whether to allow slavery

In spite of these measures, debate raged each time a new state prepared to enter the union.

## Gadsden Purchase and the 1853 Post-War Treaty with Mexico

After the Mexican-American war, a **second treaty** in 1853 determined hundreds of miles of America's southwest borders. In 1854, the **Gadsden Purchase** was finalized, providing even more territory to aid in the building of the transcontinental railroad. This purchase added what would eventually become the southernmost regions of Arizona and New Mexico to the growing nation. The modern outline of the United States was by this time nearly complete.

## Kansas-Nebraska Act Trigger of Additional Conflict

With the creation of the Kansas and Nebraska territories in 1854, another debate began. Congress allowed popular sovereignty in these territories, but slavery opponents argued that the Missouri Compromise had already made slavery illegal in this region. In Kansas, two separate governments arose, one pro-slavery and one anti-slavery. Conflict between the two factions rose to violence, leading Kansas to gain the nickname of "**Bleeding Kansas**."

**Review Video: Sectional Crisis: The Kansas-Nebraska Act**
Visit mometrix.com/academy and enter code: 982119

## Early Leaders in the Women's Rights Movement

The women's rights movement began in the 1840s, with leaders including Elizabeth Cady Stanton, Sojourner Truth, Ernestine Rose, and Lucretia Mott. In 1869, Elizabeth Cady Stanton and Susan B. Anthony formed the **National Woman Suffrage Association**, fighting for women's right to vote.

In 1848, in Seneca Falls, the first women's rights convention was held, with about 300 attendees. The two-day **Seneca Falls Convention** discussed the rights of women to vote (suffrage) as well as equal treatment in careers, legal proceedings, etc. The convention produced a "Declaration of Sentiments," which outlined a plan for women to attain the rights they deserved. **Frederick**

**Douglass** supported the women's rights movement, as well as the abolition movement. In fact, women's rights and abolition movements often went hand-in-hand during this time period.

> **Review Video: What was the Women's Rights Movement in America?**
> Visit mometrix.com/academy and enter code: 987734

## Major Events and Developments that Brought the North and South into Conflict

The conflict between the North and South coalesced around the issue of **slavery**, but other elements contributed to the growing disagreement. Though most farmers in the South worked small farms with little or no slave labor, the huge plantations run by the South's rich depended on slaves or indentured servants to remain profitable. They had also become more dependent on **cotton**, with slave populations growing in concert with the rapid increase in cotton production. In the North, a more diverse agricultural economy and the growth of **industry** made slaves rarer. The **abolitionist movement** grew steadily, with Harriet Beecher Stowe's *Uncle Tom's Cabin* giving many an idea to rally around. A collection of anti-slavery organizations formed, with many actively working to free slaves in the South, often bringing them to the northern states or Canada.

## Dred Scott Decision

Abolitionist factions coalesced around the case of **Dred Scott**, using his case to test the country's laws regarding slavery. Scott, a slave, had been taken by his owner from Missouri, which was a slave state. He then traveled to Illinois, a free state, then on to the Minnesota Territory, also free based on the Missouri Compromise. After several years, he returned to Missouri, and his owner subsequently died. Abolitionists took Scott's case to court, stating that Scott was no longer a slave but free, since he had lived in free territory. The case went to the Supreme Court.

The Supreme Court stated that, because Scott, as a slave, was not a US citizen, his time in free states did not change his status. He also did not have the right to sue. In addition, the Court determined that the **Missouri Compromise** was unconstitutional, stating that Congress had overstepped its bounds by outlawing slavery in the territories.

> **Review Video: What was the Dred Scott Decision?**
> Visit mometrix.com/academy and enter code: 364838

## Anti-Slavery Organizations

Five anti-slavery organizations and their significance are:

- **American Colonization Society**—Protestant churches formed this group, aimed at returning black slaves to Africa. Former slaves subsequently formed Liberia, but the colony did not do well, as the region was not well-suited for agriculture.
- **American Anti-Slavery Society**—William Lloyd Garrison, a Quaker, was the major force behind this group and its newspaper, *The Liberator*.
- **Philadelphia Female Anti-Slavery Society**—this women-only group was formed by Margaretta Forten because women were not allowed to join the Anti-Slavery Society formed by her father.
- **Anti-Slavery Convention of American Women**—this group continued meeting even after pro-slavery factions burned down their original meeting place.
- **Female Vigilant Society**—this organization raised funds to help the Underground Railroad, as well as slave refugees.

## Incidents at Harper's Ferry and John Brown's Role

John Brown, an abolitionist, had participated in several anti-slavery activities, including killing five pro-slavery men in retaliation, after the sacking of Lawrence, Kansas, an anti-slavery town. He and other abolitionists also banded together to pool their funds and build a runaway slave colony.

In 1859, Brown seized a federal arsenal in **Harper's Ferry**, located in what is now West Virginia. Brown intended to seize guns and ammunition and lead a slave rebellion. **Robert E. Lee** captured Brown and 21 followers, who were subsequently tried and hanged. While Northerners took the executions as an indication that the government supported slavery, Southerners were of the opinion that most of the North supported Brown and were, in general, anti-slavery.

## Presidential Candidates for the 1860 Election

The 1860 presidential candidates represented four different parties, each with a different opinion on slavery:

- **John Breckinridge**, representing the Southern Democrats, was pro-slavery but urged compromise to preserve the Union.
- **Abraham Lincoln**, of the Republican Party, was anti-slavery.
- **Stephen Douglas**, of the Northern Democrats, felt that the issue should be determined locally, on a state-by-state basis.
- **John Bell**, of the Constitutional Union Party, focused primarily on keeping the Union intact.

In the end, Abraham Lincoln won both the popular and electoral election. Southern states, who had sworn to secede from the Union if Lincoln was elected, did so, led by South Carolina. Shortly thereafter, the Civil War began when Confederate shots were fired on **Fort Sumter** in Charleston.

## North vs. South in the Civil War

The Northern states had significant advantages, including:

- **Larger population**—the North consisted of 24 states, while the South had 11.
- **Better transportation and finances**—with railroads primarily in the North, supply chains were much more dependable, as was overseas trade.
- **Raw materials**—the North held the majority of America's gold, as well as iron, copper, and other minerals vital to wartime.

The South's advantages included the following:

- **Better-trained military officers**—many of the Southern officers were West Point trained and had commanded in the Mexican and Indian wars.
- **Familiarity with weapons**—the climate and lifestyle of the South meant most of the people were experienced with both guns and horses. The industrial North had less extensive experience.
- **Defensive position**—the South felt that victory was guaranteed, since they were protecting their own lands, while the North would be invading.
- **Well-defined goals**—the South fought an ideological war to be allowed to govern themselves and preserve their way of life. The North originally fought to preserve the Union and later to free the slaves.

**Review Video: The Civil War: A North vs South Overview**
Visit mometrix.com/academy and enter code: 370788

### Benefit of the Emancipation Proclamation on the Union's Military Strategy

The Emancipation Proclamation, issued by President Lincoln on January 1, 1863, freed all slaves in **Confederate states** that were still in rebellion against the Union. While the original proclamation did not free any slaves in the states actually under Union control, it did set a precedent for the emancipation of slaves as the war progressed.

The **Emancipation Proclamation** worked in the Union's favor, as many freed slaves and other black troops joined the **Union Army**. Almost 200,000 blacks fought in the Union army, and over 10,000 served in the navy. By the end of the war, over 4 million slaves had been freed, and in 1865 slavery was abolished in the **13th amendment** to the Constitution.

**Review Video: The Civil War: The Emancipation Proclamation**
Visit mometrix.com/academy and enter code: 181778

### Major Events of the Civil War

Six major events of the Civil War and their outcomes or significance are:

- The **First Battle of Bull Run** (July 21, 1861)—this was the first major land battle of the war. Observers, expecting to enjoy an entertaining skirmish, set up picnics nearby. Instead, they found themselves witness to a bloodbath. Union forces were defeated, and the battle set the course of the Civil War as long, bloody, and costly.
- The **Capture of Fort Henry** by Ulysses S. Grant—this battle in February of 1862 marked the Union's first major victory.
- The **Battle of Gettysburg** (July 1-3, 1863)—often seen as the turning point of the war, Gettysburg also saw the largest number of casualties of the war, with over 50,000 dead, wounded, or missing. Robert E. Lee was defeated, and the Confederate army, significantly crippled, withdrew.
- The **Overland Campaign** (May and June of 1864)—Grant, now in command of all the Union armies, led this high casualty campaign that eventually positioned the Union for victory.
- **Sherman's March to the Sea**—William Tecumseh Sherman, in May of 1864, conquered Atlanta. He then continued to Savannah, destroying vast amounts of property as he went.
- Following Lee's defeat at the Appomattox Courthouse, General Grant accepted **Lee's surrender** in the home of Wilmer McLean in Appomattox, Virginia on April 9, 1865.

### Circumstances of Lincoln's Assassination

The Civil War ended with the surrender of the South on April 9, 1865. Five days later, Lincoln and his wife, Mary, went to the play *Our American Cousin* at the Ford Theater. John Wilkes Booth, who did not know that the war was over, did his part in a plot to help the Confederacy by shooting Lincoln. He was carried from the theater to a nearby house, where he died the next morning. Booth was tracked down and killed by Union soldiers twelve days later.

**Review Video: Overview of the Civil War**
Visit mometrix.com/academy and enter code: 239557

### Goals of Reconstruction and the Freedmen's Bureau

In the aftermath of the Civil War, the South was left in chaos. From 1865 to 1877, government on all levels worked to help restore order to the South, ensure civil rights to the freed slaves, and bring the Confederate states back into the Union. This became known as the **Reconstruction period.** In 1866, Congress passed the **Reconstruction Acts**, placing former Confederate states under military rule and stating the grounds for readmission into the Union.

The **Freedmen's Bureau** was formed to help freedmen both with basic necessities like food and clothing and also with employment and finding of family members who had been separated during the war. Many in the South felt the Freedmen's Bureau worked to set freed slaves against their former owners. The Bureau was intended to help former slaves become self-sufficient, and to keep them from falling prey to those who would take advantage of them. It eventually closed due to lack of funding and to violence from the **Ku Klux Klan**.

## Policies of the Radical and Moderate Republicans

The **Radical Republicans** wished to treat the South quite harshly after the war. **Thaddeus Stevens**, the House Leader, suggested that the Confederate states be treated as if they were territories again, with ten years of military rule and territorial government before they would be readmitted. He also wanted to give all black men the right to vote. Former Confederate soldiers would be required to swear they had never supported the Confederacy (knows as the "Ironclad Oath") in order to be granted full rights as American citizens.

In contrast, the **moderate Republicans** wanted only black men who were literate or who had served as Union troops to be able to vote. All Confederate soldiers except troop leaders would also be able to vote. Before his death, **Lincoln** had favored a more moderate approach to Reconstruction, hoping this approach might bring some states back into the Union before the end of the war.

## Phases of Reconstruction

The three phases of Reconstruction are:

- **Presidential Reconstruction**—largely driven by President Andrew Johnson's policies, the presidential phase of Reconstruction was lenient on the South and allowed continued discrimination against and control over blacks.
- **Congressional Reconstruction**—Congress, controlled largely by Radical Republicans, took a different stance, providing a wider range of civil rights for blacks and greater control over Southern government. Congressional Reconstruction is marked by military control of the former Confederate States.
- **Redemption**—gradually, the Confederate states were readmitted into the Union. During this time, white Democrats took over the government of most of the South. In 1877, President Rutherford Hayes withdrew the last federal troops from the South.

## Carpetbaggers and Scalawags

The chaos in the South attracted a number of people seeking to fill the power vacuums and take advantage of the economic disruption. **Scalawags** were southern whites who aligned with freedmen to take over local governments. Many in the South who could have filled political offices refused to take the necessary oath required to grant them the right to vote, leaving many opportunities for Scalawags and others. **Carpetbaggers** were Northerners who traveled to the South for various reasons. Some provided assistance, while others sought to make money or to acquire political power during this chaotic period.

## Black Codes and the Civil Rights Bill

The Black Codes were proposed to control freed slaves. They would not be allowed to bear arms, assemble, serve on juries, or testify against whites. Schools would be segregated, and unemployed blacks could be arrested and forced to work. The **Civil Rights Act** countered these codes, providing much wider rights for the freed slaves.

**Andrew Johnson**, who became president after Lincoln's death, supported the Black Codes and vetoed the Civil Rights Act in 1865 and again in 1866. The second time, Congress overrode his veto, and it became law.

Two years later, Congress voted to **impeach** Johnson, the culmination of tensions between Congress and the president. He was tried and came within a single vote of being convicted, but ultimately was acquitted and finished his term in office.

## Purpose of the Thirteenth, Fourteenth, and Fifteenth Amendments

The Thirteenth, Fourteenth and Fifteenth Amendments were all passed shortly after the end of the Civil War:

- The **Thirteenth Amendment** was ratified by the states on December 6, 1865. This amendment prohibited slavery in the United States.
- The **Fourteenth Amendment** overturned the Dred Scott decision and was ratified July 9, 1868. American citizenship was redefined: a citizen was any person born or naturalized in the US, with all citizens guaranteed equal legal protection by all states. It also guaranteed citizens of any race the right to file a lawsuit or serve on a jury.
- The **Fifteenth Amendment** was ratified on February 3, 1870. It states that no citizen of the United States can be denied the right to vote based on race, color, or previous status as a slave.

## Developments in Transportation

As America expanded its borders, it also developed new technology to travel the rapidly growing country. Roads and railroads traversed the nation, with the **Transcontinental Railroad** eventually allowing travel from one coast to the other. Canals and steamboats simplified water travel and made shipping easier and less expensive. The **Erie Canal** (1825) connected the Great Lakes to the Hudson River. Other canals connected other major waterways, further facilitating transportation and the shipment of goods.

## Transcontinental Railroad

In 1869, the **Union Pacific Railroad** completed the first section of a planned **transcontinental railroad**. This section went from Omaha, Nebraska to Sacramento, California. Ninety percent of the workers were Chinese, working in very dangerous conditions for very low pay. With the rise of the railroad, products were much more easily transported across the country. While this was positive overall for industry throughout the country, it was often damaging to family farmers, who found themselves paying high shipping costs for smaller supply orders while larger companies received major discounts.

## Measures to Limit Immigration in the 19th Century

In 1870, the **Naturalization Act** put limits on US citizenship, allowing full citizenship only to whites and those of African descent. The **Chinese Exclusion Act of 1882** put limits on Chinese immigration. The **Immigration Act of 1882** taxed immigrants, charging 50 cents per person. These funds helped pay administrative costs for regulating immigration. **Ellis Island** opened in 1892 as a processing center for those arriving in New York. The year 1921 saw the **Emergency Quota Act** passed, also known as the **Johnson Quota Act**, which severely limited the number of immigrants allowed into the country.

## AGRICULTURE IN THE 19TH CENTURY

### *TECHNOLOGICAL ADVANCES IN AGRICULTURAL CHANGES*

During the mid-1800s, irrigation techniques improved significantly. Advances occurred in cultivation and breeding, as well as fertilizer use and crop rotation. In the Great Plains, also known as the Great American Desert, the dense soil was finally cultivated with steel plows. In 1892, gasoline-powered tractors arrived, and they were widely used by 1900. Other advancements in agriculture's toolset included barbed wire fences, combines, silos, deep-water wells, and the cream separator.

### *MAJOR ACTIONS THAT HELPED IMPROVE AGRICULTURE*

Four major government actions that helped improve US agriculture in the 19th century are:

- The **Department of Agriculture** came into being in 1862, working for the interests of farmers and ranchers across the country.
- The **Morrill Land-Grant Acts** were a series of acts passed between 1862 and 1890, allowing land-grant colleges.
- In conjunction with land-grant colleges, the **Hatch Act of 1887** brought agriculture experiment stations into the picture, helping discover new farming techniques.
- In 1914, the **Smith-Lever Act** provided cooperative programs to help educate people about food, home economics, community development, and agriculture. Related agriculture extension programs helped farmers increase crop production to feed the rapidly growing nation.

## INVENTORS FROM THE 1800S

Major inventors from the 1800s and their inventions include:

- Alexander Graham Bell—the telephone
- Orville and Wilbur Wright—the airplane
- Richard Gatling—the machine gun
- Walter Hunt, Elias Howe, and Isaac Singer—the sewing machine
- Nikola Tesla—alternating current motor
- George Eastman—the Kodak camera
- Thomas Edison—light bulbs, motion pictures, the phonograph
- Samuel Morse—the telegraph
- Charles Goodyear—vulcanized rubber
- Cyrus McCormick—the reaper
- George Westinghouse—the transformer, the air brake

This was an active period for invention, with about 700,000 patents registered between 1860 and 1900.

## GILDED AGE

The time period from the end of the Civil War to the beginning of the First World War is often referred to as the **Gilded Age**, or the **Second Industrial Revolution**. The US was changing from an agricultural-based economy to an **industrial economy**, with rapid growth accompanying the shift. In addition, the country itself was expanding, spreading into the seemingly unlimited west.

This time period saw the beginning of banks, department stores, chain stores, and trusts—all familiar features of the modern-day landscape. Cities also grew rapidly, and large numbers of immigrants arrived in the country, swelling the urban ranks.

**Review Video: The Gilded Age: An Overview**
Visit mometrix.com/academy and enter code: 684770

**Review Video: The Gilded Age: Chinese Immigration**
Visit mometrix.com/academy and enter code: 624166

## Factors Leading to the Development of the Populist Party

A major **recession** struck the United States during the 1890s, with crop prices falling dramatically. **Drought** compounded the problems, leaving many American farmers in crippling debt. The **Farmers' Alliance** formed in 1875, drawing the rural poor into a single political entity.

Recession also affected the more industrial parts of the country. The **Knights of Labor**, formed in 1869 by **Uriah Stephens**, was able to unite workers into a union to protect their rights. Dissatisfied by views espoused by industrialists, the Farmers Alliance and the Knights of Labor, joined to form the **Populist Party**, also known as the People's Party, in 1892. Some of the elements of the party's platform included:

- National currency
- Graduated income tax
- Government ownership of railroads as well as telegraph and telephone systems
- Secret ballots for voting
- Immigration restriction
- Single-term limits for president and vice-president

The Populist Party was in favor of decreasing elitism and making the voice of the common man more easily heard in the political process.

## Growth of the Labor Movement Through the Late 19th Century

One of the first large, well-organized strikes occurred in 1892. Called the **Homestead Strike**, it occurred when the Amalgamated Association of Iron and Steel Workers struck against the Carnegie Steel Company. Gunfire ensued, and Carnegie was able to eliminate the plant's union. In 1894, workers in the American Railway Union, led by Eugene Debs, initiated the **Pullman Strike** after the Pullman Palace Car Co. cut their wages by 28 percent. President Grover Cleveland called in troops to break up the strike on the grounds that it interfered with mail delivery. Mary Harris "Mother" Jones organized the **Children's Crusade** to protest child labor. A protest march proceeded to the home of President Theodore Roosevelt in 1903. Jones also worked with the United Mine Workers of America and helped found the **Industrial Workers of the World**.

## Panic of 1893

Far from a US-centric event, the **Panic of 1893** was an economic crisis that affected most of the globe. As a response, President Grover Cleveland repealed the **Sherman Silver Purchase Act**, afraid it had caused the downturn rather than boosting the economy as intended. The Panic led to bankruptcies, with banks and railroads going under and factory unemployment rising as high as 25 percent. In the end, the **Republican Party** regained power due to the economic crisis.

## Progressive Era

From the 1890s to the end of the First World War, **Progressives** set forth an ideology that drove many levels of society and politics. The Progressives were in favor of workers' rights and safety and wanted measures taken against waste and corruption. They felt science could help improve society and that the government could—and should—provide answers to a variety of social problems. Progressives came from a wide variety of backgrounds but were united in their desire to improve society.

> **Review Video: The Progressive Era**
> Visit mometrix.com/academy and enter code: 722394

## Muckrakers and the Progressive Movement

"Muckrakers" was a term used to identify aggressive investigative journalists who exposed scandals, corruption, and many other wrongs in late 19th-century society. Among these intrepid writers were:

- **Ida Tarbell**—she exposed John D. Rockefeller's Standard Oil Trust.
- **Jacob Riis**—a photographer, he brought the living conditions of the poor in New York to the public's attention.
- **Lincoln Steffens**—he worked to expose political corruption in municipal government.
- **Upton Sinclair**—his book *The Jungle* led to reforms in the meat-packing industry.

Through the work of these journalists, many new policies came into being, including workmen's compensation, child labor laws, and trust-busting.

## Government Dealings with Native Americans Through the End of the 19th Century

America's westward expansion led to conflict and violent confrontations with Native Americans such as the **Battle of Little Bighorn**. In 1876, the American government ordered all Native Americans to relocate to reservations. Lack of compliance led to the **Dawes Act** in 1887, which ordered assimilation rather than separation: Native Americans were offered American citizenship and a piece of their tribal land if they would accept the lot chosen by the government and live on it separately from the tribe. This act remained in effect until 1934. Reformers also forced Native American children to attend **boarding schools**, where they were not allowed to speak their native language and were immersed into a Euro-American culture and religion. Children were often abused in these schools and were indoctrinated to abandon their identity as Native Americans.

In 1890, the massacre at **Wounded Knee**, accompanied by Geronimo's surrender, led the Native Americans to work to preserve their culture rather than fight for their lands.

> **Review Video: Government Dealings with Native Americans Through the End of the 19th Century**
> Visit mometrix.com/academy and enter code: 635645

## Role of Native Americans in Wartime Through the Beginning of the 20th Century

The **Spanish-American War** (1898) saw a number of Native Americans serving with Teddy Roosevelt in the Rough Riders. Apache scouts accompanied General John J. Pershing to Mexico, hoping to find **Pancho Villa**. More than 17,000 Native Americans were drafted into service for

**World War I**, though at the time, they were not considered legal citizens. In 1924, Native Americans were finally granted official citizenship by the **Indian Citizenship Act**.

After decades of relocation, forced assimilation, and genocide, the number of Native Americans in the US has greatly declined. Though many Native Americans have chosen—or have been forced—to assimilate, about 300 reservations exist today, with most of their inhabitants living in abject poverty.

**Review Video: Role of Native Americans in Wartime Through the Beginning of the 20th Century**
Visit mometrix.com/academy and enter code: 419128

### Events Leading up to the Spanish-American War

Spain had controlled **Cuba** since the 15th century. Over the centuries, the Spanish had quashed a variety of revolts. In 1886, slavery ended in Cuba, and another revolt was rising.

In the meantime, the US had expressed interest in Cuba, offering Spain $130 million for the island in 1853, during Franklin Pierce's presidency. In 1898, the Cuban revolt was underway. In spite of various factions supporting the Cubans, the US President, William McKinley, refused to recognize the rebellion, preferring negotiation over involvement in war. Then, the *Maine*, a US battleship in Havana Harbor, was blown up, killing 266 crew members. The US declared war two months later, and the war ended with a **Spanish surrender** in less than four months.

## American History 1899 to Present

### Influence of Big Stick Diplomacy on American Foreign Policy in Latin America

Theodore Roosevelt's famous quote, "Speak softly and carry a big stick," is supposedly of African origins, at least according to Roosevelt. He used this proverb to justify expanded involvement in foreign affairs during his tenure as President. The US military was deployed to protect American interests in **Latin America**. Roosevelt also worked to maintain an equal or greater influence in Latin America than those held by European interests. As a result, the US Navy grew larger, and the US generally became more involved in foreign affairs. Roosevelt felt that if any country was left vulnerable to control by Europe due to economic issues or political instability, the US had not only a right to intervene but was **obligated** to do so. This led to US involvement in Cuba, Nicaragua, Haiti, and the Dominican Republic over several decades leading into the First and Second World Wars.

### Importance of the Panama Canal

Initial work began on the **Panama Canal** in 1881, though the idea had been discussed since the 1500s. The canal greatly reduces the length and time needed to sail from one ocean to the other by connecting the Atlantic to the Pacific through the Isthmus of Panama, which joins South America to North America. Before the canal was built, travelers had to sail around the entire perimeter of South America to reach the West Coast of the US. The French began the work after successfully completing the **Suez Canal**, which connected the Mediterranean Sea to the Red Sea. However, due to disease and high expense, the work moved slowly, and after eight years, the company went bankrupt, suspending work. The US purchased the holdings, and the first ship sailed through the canal in 1914. The Panama Canal was constructed as a lock-and-lake canal, with ships lifted on locks to travel from one lake to another over the rugged, mountainous terrain. In order to maintain control of the Canal Zone, the US assisted Panama in its battle for independence from **Colombia**.

### Taft's Dollar Diplomacy vs. Roosevelt's Diplomatic Theories

During William Howard Taft's presidency, Taft instituted "**Dollar Diplomacy**." This approach was America's effort to influence Latin America and East Asia through economic rather than military means. Taft saw past efforts in these areas to be political and warlike, while his efforts focused on peaceful economic goals. His justification of the policy was to protect the **Panama Canal**, which was vital to US trade interests.

In spite of Taft's assurance that Dollar Diplomacy was a peaceful approach, many interventions proved violent. During Latin American revolts, such as those in **Nicaragua**, the US sent troops to settle the revolutions. Afterward, bankers moved in to help support the new leaders through loans. Dollar Diplomacy continued until 1913, when Woodrow Wilson was elected president.

### Growth of Civil Rights for African Americans

Marcus Garvey founded the **Universal Negro Improvement Association and African Communities League (UNIA-ACL)**, which became a large and active organization focused on building black nationalism. In 1909, the **National Association for the Advancement of Colored People (NAACP)** came into being, working to defeat Jim Crow laws. The NAACP also helped prevent racial segregation from becoming federal law, fought against lynchings, helped black soldiers in WWI become officers, and helped defend the Scottsboro Boys, who were unjustly accused of rape.

### Wilson's Approach to International Diplomacy

Turning away from Taft's "Dollar Diplomacy," Wilson instituted a foreign policy he referred to as "**moral diplomacy**." This approach still influences American foreign policy today.

Wilson felt that **representative government and democracy** in all countries would lead to worldwide stability. Democratic governments, he felt, would be less likely to threaten American interests. He also saw the US and Great Britain as the great role models in this area, as well as champions of world peace and self-government. Free trade and international commerce would allow the US to speak out regarding world events.

Main elements of Wilson's policies included:

- Maintaining a strong military
- Promoting democracy throughout the world
- Expanding international trade to boost the American economy

### Provisions of the Sixteenth, Seventeenth, Eighteenth, and Nineteenth Amendments

The early 20th century saw several amendments made to the US Constitution:

- The **Sixteenth Amendment** (1913) established a federal income tax.
- The **Seventeenth Amendment** (1913) allowed popular election of senators.
- The **Eighteenth Amendment** (1919) prohibited the sale, production, and transportation of alcohol. This amendment was later repealed by the Twenty-first Amendment.
- The **Nineteenth Amendment** (1920) gave women the right to vote.

These amendments largely grew out of the Progressive Era, as many citizens worked to improve American society.

## Goals of the Anti-Defamation League

In 1913, the Anti-Defamation League was formed to prevent anti-Semitic behavior and practices. Its actions also worked to prevent all forms of racism and to prevent individuals from being discriminated against for any reason involving their race. They spoke against the Ku Klux Klan, as well as other racist or anti-Semitic organizations. This organization still works to fight discrimination against all minorities.

## Role of the Federal Trade Commission in Eliminating Trusts

**Muckrakers** such as Ida Tarbell and Lincoln Steffens brought to light the damaging trend of trusts—huge corporations working to monopolize areas of commerce so they could control prices and distribution. The **Sherman Antitrust Act** and the **Clayton Antitrust Act** set out guidelines for competition among corporations and set out to eliminate these trusts. The **Federal Trade Commission** was formed in 1914 in order to enforce antitrust measures and ensure that companies were operated fairly and did not create controlling monopolies.

## Major Events of World War I

World War I occurred from 1914 to 1918 and was fought largely in Europe. Triggered by the assassination of Austrian Archduke Franz Ferdinand, the war rapidly escalated. At the beginning of the conflict, Woodrow Wilson declared the US neutral. Major events influencing US involvement included:

- **Sinking of the *Lusitania***—the British passenger liner RMS *Lusitania* was sunk by a German U-boat in 1915. Among the 1,000 civilian victims were over 100 American citizens. Outraged by this act, many Americans began to push for US involvement in the war, using the *Lusitania* as a rallying cry.
- **German U-boat aggression**—Wilson continued to keep the US out of the war, using as his 1916 reelection slogan, "He kept us out of war." While he continued to work toward an end of the war, German U-boats began to indiscriminately attack American and Canadian merchant ships carrying supplies to Germany's enemies in Europe.
- **Zimmerman Telegram** —the final event that brought the US into World War I was the interception of the Zimmerman Telegram (also known as the Zimmerman Note). In this telegram, Germany proposed forming an alliance with Mexico if the US entered the war.

## Efforts in the US During World War I Supporting the War Effort

American **railroads** came under government control in December 1917. The widespread system was consolidated into a single system, with each region assigned a director. This greatly increased the efficiency of the railroad system, allowing the railroads to supply both domestic and military needs. Control returned to private ownership in 1920. In 1918, **telegraph, telephone, and cable services** also came under Federal control, to be returned to private management the next year. The **American Red Cross** supported the war effort by knitting clothes for Army and Navy troops. They also helped supply hospital and refugee clothing and surgical dressings. Over 8 million people participated in this effort. To generate wartime funds, the US government sold **Liberty Bonds**. In four issues, they sold nearly $25 billion—more than one-fifth of Americans purchased them. After the war, a fifth bond drive was held but sold "**Victory Liberty Bonds**."

**Review Video: WWI Overview**
Visit mometrix.com/academy and enter code: 659767

## Influence of Wilson's Fourteen Points on the Final Peace Treaties that Ended World War I

President Woodrow Wilson proposed **Fourteen Points** as the basis for a peace settlement to end the war. Presented to the US Congress in January 1918, the Fourteen Points included:

- Five points outlining **general ideals**
- Eight points to resolve **immediate problems** of political and territorial nature
- One point proposing an **organization of nations** (the League of Nations) with the intent of maintaining world peace

In November of that same year, Germany agreed to an **armistice**, assuming the final treaty would be based on the Fourteen Points. However, during the peace conference in Paris 1919, there was much disagreement, leading to a final agreement that punished Germany and the other Central Powers much more than originally intended. Henry Cabot Lodge, who had become the Foreign Relations Committee chairman in 1918, wanted an unconditional surrender from Germany and was concerned about the article in the **Treaty of Versailles** that gave the League of Nations power to declare war without a vote from the US Congress. A **League of Nations** was included in the Treaty of Versailles at Wilson's insistence. The Senate rejected the Treaty of Versailles, and in the end, Wilson refused to concede to Lodge's demands. As a result, the US did not join the League of Nations.

## Origins of the Red Scare

World War I created many jobs, but after the war ended, these jobs disappeared, leaving many unemployed. In the wake of these employment changes, the **International Workers of the World** and the **Socialist Party**, headed by Eugene Debs, became more and more visible. Workers initiated strikes in an attempt to regain the favorable working conditions that had been put into place before the war. Unfortunately, many of these strikes became violent, and the actions were blamed on "Reds," or Communists, for trying to spread their views into America. With the recent Bolshevik Revolution in Russia, many Americans feared a similar revolution might occur in the US. The **Red Scare** ensued, with many individuals jailed for supposedly holding communist, anarchist, or socialist beliefs.

## Major Changes and Events that Took Place in America During the 1920s

The post-war 1920s saw many Americans moving from the farm to the city, with growing prosperity in the US. The **Roaring Twenties**, or the **Jazz Age**, was driven largely by growth in the automobile and entertainment industries. Individuals like Charles Lindbergh, the first aviator to make a solo flight across the Atlantic Ocean, added to the American admiration of individual accomplishment. Telephone lines, distribution of electricity, highways, the radio, and other inventions brought great changes to everyday life.

**Review Video: 1920's**
Visit mometrix.com/academy and enter code: 124996

## Major Cultural Movements of the 1920s Influenced by African Americans

The **Harlem Renaissance** saw a number of African-American artists settling in Harlem in New York. This community produced a number of well-known artists and writers, including Langston Hughes, Nella Larsen, Zora Neale Hurston, Claude McKay, Countee Cullen, and Jean Toomer. The growth of jazz, also largely driven by African Americans, defined the **Jazz Age**. Its unconventional, improvisational style matched the growing sense of optimism and exploration of the decade. Originating as an offshoot of the blues, jazz began in New Orleans. Some significant jazz musicians were Duke Ellington, Louis Armstrong, and Jelly Roll Morton. **Big Band** and **Swing Jazz** also developed in the 1920s. Well-known musicians of this movement included Bing Crosby, Frank Sinatra, Count Basie, Benny Goodman, Billie Holiday, Ella Fitzgerald, and The Dorsey Brothers.

## American Civil Liberties Union

The American Civil Liberties Union (**ACLU**), founded in 1920, grew from the American Union Against Militarism. The ACLU helped conscientious objectors avoid going to war during WWI, and also helped those being prosecuted under the **Espionage Act** (1917) and the **Sedition Act** (1918), many of whom were immigrants. Their major goals were to protect immigrants and other citizens who were threatened with prosecution for their political beliefs, and to support labor unions, which were also under threat by the government during the Red Scare.

## Provisions and Importance of the National Origins Act of 1924

The National Origins Act (Johnson-Reed Act) placed limitations on **immigration**. The number of immigrants allowed into the US was based on the population of each nationality of immigrants who were living in the country in 1890. Only two percent of each nationality's 1890 population numbers were allowed to immigrate. This led to great disparities between immigrants from various nations, and Asian immigration was not allowed at all. Some of the impetus behind the Johnson-Reed Act came as a result of paranoia following the **Russian Revolution**. Fear of communist influences in the US led to a general fear of immigrants.

## Ku Klux Klan

In 1866, Confederate Army veterans came together to fight against Reconstruction in the South, forming a group called the **Ku Klux Klan (KKK)**. With white supremacist beliefs, including anti-Semitism, nativism, anti-Catholicism, and overt racism, this organization relied heavily on violence to get its message across. In 1915, they grew again in power, using a film called *The Birth of a Nation*, by D.W. Griffith, to spread their ideas. In the 1920s, the reach of the KKK spread far into the north and midwest, and members controlled a number of state governments. Its membership and power began to decline during the Great Depression but experienced a resurgence later.

## Roosevelt's New Deal

The **Great Depression**, which began in 1929 with the stock market crash, grew out of several factors that had developed over the previous years, including:

- Growing economic disparity between the rich and middle classes, with the rich amassing wealth much more quickly than the lower classes
- Disparity in economic distribution in industries
- Growing use of credit, leading to an inflated demand for some goods
- Government support of new industries rather than agriculture
- Risky stock market investments, leading to the stock market crash

Additional factors contributing to the Depression also included the **Labor Day Hurricane** in the Florida Keys (1935) and the **Great Hurricane of 1938** in New England, along with the **Dust Bowl** in the Great Plains, which destroyed crops and resulted in the displacement of as many as 2.5 million people.

**Review Video: What Caused the Great Depression?**
Visit mometrix.com/academy and enter code: 635912

**Franklin D. Roosevelt** was elected president in 1932 with his promise of a "**New Deal**" for Americans. His goals were to provide government work programs to provide jobs, wages, and relief to numerous workers throughout the beleaguered US. Congress gave Roosevelt almost free rein to produce relief legislation. The goals of this legislation were:

- **Relief**—creating jobs for the high numbers of unemployed
- **Recovery**—stimulating the economy through the National Recovery Administration
- **Reform**—passing legislation to prevent future, similar economic crashes

The Roosevelt Administration also passed legislation regarding ecological issues, including the Soil Conservation Service, aimed at preventing another Dust Bowl.

## Roosevelt's Alphabet Organizations

So-called "alphabet organizations" set up during Roosevelt's administration included:

- **Civilian Conservation Corps** (CCC)—provided jobs in the forestry service
- **Agricultural Adjustment Administration** (AAA)—increased agricultural income by adjusting both production and prices
- **Tennessee Valley Authority** (TVA)—organized projects to build dams in the Tennessee River for flood control and production of electricity, resulting in increased productivity for industries in the area, and easier navigation of the Tennessee River
- **Public Works Administration** (PWA) and Civil Works Administration (CWA)—provided a multitude of jobs, initiating over 34,000 projects
- **Works Progress Administration** (WPA)—helped unemployed persons to secure employment on government work projects or elsewhere

## Actions Taken During the Roosevelt Administration to Prevent Future Crashes

The Roosevelt administration passed several laws and established several institutions to initiate the "reform" portion of the New Deal, including:

- **Glass-Steagall Act**—separated investment from commercial banking
- **Securities Exchange Commission (SEC)**—helped regulate Wall Street investment practices, making them less dangerous to the overall economy
- **Wagner Act**—provided worker and union rights to improve relations between employees and employers
- **Social Security Act of 1935**—provided pensions as well as unemployment insurance

Other actions focused on insuring bank deposits and adjusting the value of American currency. Most of these regulatory agencies and government policies and programs still exist today.

## Major Regulations Regarding Labor After the Great Depression

Three major regulations regarding labor that were passed after the Great Depression are:

- The **Wagner Act** (1935)—also known as the National Labor Relations Act, it established that unions were legal, protected members of unions, and required collective bargaining. This act was later amended by the Taft-Hartley Act of 1947 and the Landrum-Griffin Act of 1959, which further clarified certain elements.
- **Davis-Bacon Act** (1931)—provided fair compensation for contractors and subcontractors.
- **Walsh-Healey Act** (1936)—established a minimum wage, child labor laws, safety standards, and overtime pay.

## Interventionist and Isolationist Approaches in World War II

When war broke out in Europe in 1939, President Roosevelt stated that the US would remain **neutral**. However, his overall approach was considered "**interventionist**," as he was willing to provide aid to the Allies without actually entering the conflict. Thus, the US supplied a wide variety of war materials to the Allied nations in the early years of the war.

**Isolationists** believed the US should not provide any aid to the Allies, including supplies. They felt Roosevelt, by assisting the Allies, was leading the US into a war for which it was not prepared. Led by Charles Lindbergh, the Isolationists believed that any involvement in the European conflict endangered the US by weakening its national defense.

## Sequence of Events that Led the US to Declare War and Enter World War II

In 1937, Japan invaded China, prompting the US to eventually halt exports to Japan. Roosevelt also did not allow Japanese interests to withdraw money held in US banks. In 1941, **General Tojo** rose to power as the Japanese prime minister. Recognizing America's ability to bring a halt to Japan's expansion, he authorized the bombing of **Pearl Harbor** on December 7. The US responded by declaring war on Japan. Partially because of the **Tripartite Pact** among the Axis Powers, Germany and Italy then declared war on the US, later followed by Bulgaria, Hungary, and other Axis nations.

**Review Video: World War II Overview**
Visit mometrix.com/academy and enter code: 759402

## Occurrences of World War II that Led to the Surrender of Germany

In 1941, **Hitler** violated the non-aggression pact he had signed with Stalin two years earlier by invading the USSR. **Stalin** then joined the **Allies**. Stalin, Roosevelt, and Winston Churchill planned to defeat Germany first, then Japan, bringing the war to an end.

In 1942-1943, the Allies drove **Axis** forces out of Africa. In addition, the Germans were soundly defeated at Stalingrad.

The **Italian Campaign** involved Allied operations in Italy between July 1943 and May 1945, including Italy's liberation. On June 6, 1944, known as **D-Day**, the Allies invaded France at Normandy. Soviet troops moved on the eastern front at the same time, driving German forces back. By April 25, 1945, Berlin was surrounded by Soviet troops. On May 7, Germany surrendered.

## Major Events of World War II that Led to the Surrender of Japan

War continued with **Japan** after Germany's surrender. Japanese forces had taken a large portion of Southeast Asia and the Western Pacific, all the way to the Aleutian Islands in Alaska. **General Doolittle** bombed several Japanese cities while American troops scored a victory at Midway. Additional fighting in the Battle of the Coral Sea further weakened Japan's position. As a final blow, the US dropped two **atomic bombs** on Japan, one on Hiroshima and the other on Nagasaki. This was the first time atomic bombs had been used in warfare, and the devastation was horrific and demoralizing. Japan surrendered on September 2, 1945, which became **V-J Day** in the US.

## Significance of the 442nd Regimental Combat Team, the Tuskegee Airmen, and the Navajo Code Talkers during World War II

The 442nd Regimental Combat Team consisted of Japanese-Americans fighting in Europe for the US. The most highly decorated unit per member in US history, they suffered a 93% casualty rate during the war. The **Tuskegee Airmen** were African American aviators, the first black Americans allowed to fly for the military. In spite of being ineligible to become official navy pilots, they flew over 15,000 missions and were highly decorated. The **Navajo Code Talkers** were native Navajo who used their traditional language to transmit information among Allied forces. Because Navajo is a language and not simply a code, the Axis powers were never able to translate it. The use of Navajo Code Talkers to transmit information was instrumental in the taking of Iwo Jima and other major victories of the war.

## Circumstances and Opportunities for Women During World War II

Women served widely in the military during WWII, working in numerous positions, including the **Flight Nurses Corps**. Women also moved into the workforce while men were overseas, leading to over 19 million women in the US workforce by 1944. **Rosie the Riveter** stood as a symbol of these women and a means of recruiting others to take needed positions. Women, as well as their families left behind during wartime, also grew **Victory Gardens** to help provide food.

## Importance of the Atomic Bomb During World War II

The atomic bomb, developed during WWII, was the most powerful bomb ever invented. A single bomb, carried by a single plane, held enough power to destroy an entire city. This devastating effect was demonstrated with the bombing of **Hiroshima** and **Nagasaki** in 1945 in what later became a controversial move, but ended the war. The bombings resulted in as many as 150,000 immediate deaths and many more as time passed after the bombings, mostly due to **radiation poisoning**.

Whatever the arguments against the use of "The Bomb," the post-WWII era saw many countries develop similar weapons to match the newly expanded military power of the US. The impact of those developments and use of nuclear weapons continues to haunt international relations today.

## Importance of the Yalta Conference and the Potsdam Conference

In February 1945, Joseph Stalin, Franklin D. Roosevelt, and Winston Churchill met in Yalta to discuss the post-war treatment of the **Axis nations**, particularly Germany. Though Germany had not yet surrendered, its defeat was imminent. After Germany's official surrender, Joseph Stalin, Harry Truman (Roosevelt's successor), and Clement Attlee (replacing Churchill partway through the conference) met to formalize those plans. This meeting was called the **Potsdam Conference**. Basic provisions of these agreements included:

- Dividing Germany and Berlin into four zones of occupation
- Demilitarization of Germany
- Poland remaining under Soviet control
- Outlawing the Nazi Party
- Trials for Nazi leaders
- Relocation of numerous German citizens
- The USSR joining the United Nations, established in 1945
- Establishment of the United Nations Security Council, consisting of the US, the UK, the USSR, China, and France

## Agreements Made with Post-War Japan

**General Douglas MacArthur** led the American **military occupation of Japan** after the country surrendered. The goals of the US occupation included removing Japan's military and making the country a democracy. A 1947 constitution removed power from the emperor and gave it to the people, as well as granting voting rights to women. Japan was no longer allowed to declare war, and a group of 28 government officials were tried for war crimes. In 1951, the US finally signed a peace treaty with Japan. This treaty allowed Japan to rearm itself for purposes of self-defense but stripped the country of the empire it had built overseas.

## US Treatment of Immigrants During and After World War II

In 1940, the US passed the **Alien Registration Act**, which required all aliens older than fourteen to be fingerprinted and registered. They were also required to report changes of address within five days.

Tension between whites and Japanese immigrants in **California**, which had been building since the beginning of the century, came to a head with the bombing of **Pearl Harbor** in 1941. Believing that even those Japanese living in the US were likely to be loyal to their native country, the president ordered numerous Japanese to be arrested on suspicion of subversive action and isolated in exclusion zones known as **War Relocation Camps**. Approximately 120,000 Japanese-Americans, two-thirds of them US citizens, were sent to these camps during the war.

## General State of the US After World War II

Following WWII, the US became the strongest political power in the world, becoming a major player in world affairs and foreign policies. The US determined to stop the spread of **communism**, having named itself the "**arsenal of democracy**" during the war. In addition, America emerged with a greater sense of itself as a single, integrated nation, with many regional and economic differences diminished. The government worked for greater equality, and the growth of communications increased contact among different areas of the country. Both the aftermath of the Great Depression and the necessities of WWII had given the government greater **control** over various institutions as well as the economy. This also meant that the American government took on greater responsibility for the well-being of its citizens, both in the domestic arena, such as providing basic needs, and in protecting them from foreign threats. This increased role of providing basic necessities for all Americans has been criticized by some as "**the welfare state**."

## US Policy Toward Immigrants After World War II

Prior to WWII, the US had been limiting **immigration** for several decades. After WWII, policy shifted slightly to accommodate political refugees from Europe and elsewhere. So many people were displaced by the war that in 1946, the UN formed the **International Refugee Organization** to deal with the problem. In 1948, the US Congress passed the **Displaced Persons Act**, which allowed over 400,000 European refugees to enter the US, most of them concentration camp survivors and refugees from Eastern Europe.

In 1952, the **United States Escapee Program (USEP)** increased the quotas, allowing refugees from communist Europe to enter the US, as did the **Refugee Relief Act**, passed in 1953. At the same time, however, the **Internal Security Act of 1950** allowed deportation of declared communists, and Asians were subjected to a quota based on race, rather than country of origin. Later changes included:

- **Migration and Refugee Assistance Act** (1962)—provided aid for refugees in need
- **Immigration and Nationality Act** (1965)—ended quotas based on nation of origin
- **Immigration Reform and Control Act** (1986)—prohibited the hiring of illegal immigrants but also granted amnesty to about three million illegals already in the country

## Accomplishments of Harry S. Truman

Harry S. Truman took over the presidency from Franklin D. Roosevelt near the end of WWII. He made the final decision to drop atomic bombs on Japan and played a major role in the final decisions regarding the treatment of post-war Germany. On the domestic front, Truman initiated a 21-point plan known as the **Fair Deal**. This plan expanded Social Security, provided public housing, and made the Fair Employment Practice Committee permanent. Truman helped support Greece and

Turkey (which were under threat from the USSR), supported South Korea against communist North Korea, and helped with recovery in Western Europe. He also participated in the formation of **NATO**, the North Atlantic Treaty Organization.

## Events and Importance of the Korean War

The Korean War began in 1950 and ended in 1953. For the first time in history, a world organization—the **United Nations**—played a military role in a war. North Korea sent communist troops into South Korea, seeking to bring the entire country under communist control. The UN sent out a call to member nations, asking them to support South Korea. Truman sent troops, as did many other UN member nations. The war ended three years later with a **truce** rather than a peace treaty, and Korea remains divided at the **38th parallel north**, with communist rule remaining in the North and a democratic government ruling the South.

## Effects of US Cold War Foreign Policy Acts on the International Relationships

The following are US Cold War foreign policy acts and how they affected international relationships, especially between the US and the Soviet Union:

- **Marshall Plan**—this sent aid to war-torn Europe after WWII, largely focusing on preventing the spread of communism.
- **Containment Policy**—proposed by George F. Kennan, the containment policy focused on containing the spread of Soviet communism.
- **Truman Doctrine**—Harry S. Truman stated that the US would provide both economic and military support to any country threatened by Soviet takeover.
- **National Security Act**—passed in 1947, this act reorganized the government's military departments into the Department of Defense and created the Central Intelligence Agency and the National Security Council.

The combination of these acts led to the **Cold War**, with Soviet communists attempting to spread their influence and the US and other countries trying to contain or stop this spread.

## Accomplishments of Dwight D. Eisenhower

Eisenhower carried out a middle-of-the-road foreign policy and brought the US several steps forward in equal rights. He worked to minimize tensions during the Cold War and negotiated a peace treaty with Russia after the death of Stalin. He enforced desegregation by sending troops to Little Rock Central High School in Arkansas, as well as ordering the desegregation of the military. Organizations formed during his administration included the Department of Health, Education, and Welfare, and the National Aeronautics and Space Administration (NASA).

## Effect of the Arms Race on Post WWII International Relations

After World War II, major nations, particularly the US and USSR, rushed to develop highly advanced weapons systems such as the **atomic bomb** and later the **hydrogen bomb**. These countries seemed determined to outpace each other with the development of numerous, deadly weapons. These weapons were expensive and extremely dangerous, and it is possible that the war between US and Soviet interests remained "cold" due to the fear that one side or the other would use these powerful weapons.

## Technological Advances that Occurred Throughout the 1900s

Numerous technological advances throughout the 1900s led to more effective treatment of diseases, more efficient communication and transportation, and new means of generating power. Advances in **medicine** increased the human lifespan in developed countries, and near-instantaneous **communication** opened up a myriad of possibilities. Some of these advances include:

- Discovery of penicillin (1928)
- Supersonic air travel (1947)
- Nuclear power plants (1951)
- Orbital satellite leading to manned space flight (Sputnik, 1957)
- First man on the moon (1969)

## NATO, Warsaw Pact, and the Berlin Wall

NATO, the **North Atlantic Treaty Organization**, came into being in 1949. It essentially amounted to an agreement among the US and Western European countries that an attack on any one of these countries was to be considered an attack against the entire group. Under the influence of the Soviet Union, the Eastern European countries of the USSR, Bulgaria, East Germany, Poland, Romania, Albania, Hungary, and Czechoslovakia responded with the **Warsaw Pact**, which created a similar agreement among those nations. In 1961, a wall was built to separate communist East Berlin from democratic West Berlin. This was a literal representation of the "**Iron Curtain**" that separated the democratic and communist countries throughout the world.

## Presidency of John F. Kennedy

Although his term was cut short by his assassination, **JFK** instituted economic programs that led to a period of continuous expansion in the US unmatched since before WWII. He formed the Alliance for Progress and the Peace Corps, organizations intended to help developing nations. He also oversaw the passage of new civil rights legislation and drafted plans to attack poverty and its causes, along with support of the arts. Kennedy's presidency ended when he was assassinated by **Lee Harvey Oswald** in 1963.

## Events of the Cuban Missile Crisis

The Cuban Missile Crisis occurred in 1962, during John F. Kennedy's presidency. Russian Premier **Nikita Khrushchev** decided to place nuclear missiles in **Cuba** to protect the island from invasion by the US. An American U-2 plane flying over the island photographed the missile bases as they were being built. Tensions rose, with the US concerned about nuclear missiles so close to its shores, and the USSR concerned about American missiles that had been placed in **Turkey**. Eventually, the missile sites were removed, and a US naval blockade turned back Soviet ships carrying missiles to Cuba. During negotiations, the US agreed to remove their missiles from Turkey and agreed to sell surplus wheat to the USSR. A telephone hotline between Moscow and Washington was set up to allow instant communication between the two heads of state to prevent similar incidents in the future.

## Accomplishments of the Lyndon B. Johnson Presidency

Kennedy's vice president, **Lyndon Johnson**, assumed the presidency after Kennedy's **assassination**. He supported civil rights bills, tax cuts, and other wide-reaching legislation that Kennedy had also supported. Johnson saw America as a "**Great Society**," and enacted legislation to fight disease and poverty, renew urban areas, and support education and environmental conservation. Medicare and Medicaid were instituted under his administration. He continued Kennedy's support of space exploration, and he is also known, although less positively, for his handling of the **Vietnam War**.

## Factors that Led to the Growth of the Civil Rights Movement

In the 1950s, post-war America was experiencing a rapid growth in prosperity. However, African-Americans found themselves left behind. Following the lead of **Mahatma Gandhi**, who led similar class struggles in India, African-Americans began to demand equal rights. Major figures in this struggle included:

- **Rosa Parks**—often called the "mother of the Civil Rights Movement," her refusal to give up her seat on the bus to a white man served as a seed from which the movement grew.
- **Martin Luther King, Jr.**—the best-known leader of the movement, King drew on Gandhi's beliefs and encouraged non-violent opposition. He led a march on Washington in 1963, received the Nobel Peace Prize in 1964, and was assassinated in 1968.
- **Malcolm X**—espousing less peaceful means of change, Malcolm X became a Black Muslim and supported black nationalism.

## Policies and Legislation Enacted Expanding Minority Rights

Several major acts have been passed, particularly since WWII, to protect the rights of minorities in America. These include:

- Civil Rights Act (1964)
- Voting Rights Act (1965)
- Age Discrimination Act (1967)
- Americans with Disabilities Act (1990)

Other important movements for civil rights included a prisoner's rights movement, movements for immigrant rights, and the women's rights movement. The National Organization for Women (NOW) was established in 1966 and worked to pass the Equal Rights Amendment. The amendment was passed, but not enough states ratified it for it to become part of the US Constitution.

## Impact of Stokely Carmichael, Adam Clayton Powell, and Jesse Jackson on the Civil Rights Movement

- **Stokely Carmichael**—Carmichael originated the term "Black Power" and served as head of the Student Nonviolent Coordinating Committee. He believed in black pride and black culture and felt separate political and social institutions should be developed for blacks.
- **Adam Clayton Powell**—chairman of the Coordinating Committee for Employment, he led rent strikes and other actions, as well as a bus boycott, to increase the hiring of blacks.
- **Jesse Jackson**—Jackson was selected to head the Chicago Operation Breadbasket in 1966, and went on to organize boycotts and other actions. He also had an unsuccessful run for president.

## Events of the Civil Rights Movement

Three major events of the Civil Rights Movement are:

- **Montgomery Bus Boycott**—in 1955, Rosa Parks refused to give her seat on the bus to a white man. As a result, she was tried and convicted of disorderly conduct and of violating local ordinances. A 381-day bus boycott ensued, protesting segregation on public buses.

- **Desegregation of Little Rock**—in 1957, after the Supreme Court decision on Brown v. Board of Education, which declared "separate but equal" unconstitutional, the Arkansas school board voted to desegregate their schools. Even though Arkansas was considered progressive, its governor brought in the Arkansas National Guard to prevent nine black students from entering Central High School in Little Rock. President Eisenhower responded by federalizing the National Guard and ordering them to stand down.
- **Birmingham Campaign**—protestors organized a variety of actions such as sit-ins and an organized march to launch a voting campaign. When the City of Birmingham declared the protests illegal, the protestors, including Martin Luther King, Jr., persisted and were arrested and jailed.

## Pieces of Legislation Passed as a Result of the Civil Rights Movement

Three major pieces of legislation passed as a result of the Civil Rights movement are:

- **Brown v. Board of Education** (1954)—the Supreme Court declared that "separate but equal" accommodations and services were unconstitutional.
- **Civil Rights Act of 1964**—this declared discrimination illegal in employment, education, or public accommodation.
- **Voting Rights Act of 1965**—this act ended various activities practiced, mostly in the South, to bar blacks from exercising their voting rights. These included poll taxes and literacy tests.

## Events of the Richard Nixon Presidency

Richard Nixon is best known for the **Watergate scandal** during his presidency, but other important events marked his tenure as president, including:

- End of the Vietnam War
- Improved diplomatic relations between the US and China, and the US and the USSR
- National Environmental Policy Act passed, providing for environmental protection
- Compulsory draft ended
- Supreme Court legalized abortion in Roe v. Wade (subsequently overturned in 2022)
- Watergate

The Watergate scandal of 1972 ended Nixon's presidency. Rather than face impeachment and removal from office, he **resigned** in 1974.

## US Perspective on the Progression of the Vietnam War

After World War II, the US pledged, as part of its foreign policy, to come to the assistance of any country threatened by **communism**. When Vietnam was divided into a communist North and democratic South, much like Korea before it, the eventual attempts by the North to unify the country under Communist rule led to intervention by the US. On the home front, the **Vietnam War** became more and more unpopular politically, with Americans growing increasingly discontent with the inability of the US to achieve the goals it had set for the Asian country. When President **Richard Nixon** took office in 1969, his escalation of the war led to protests at Kent State in Ohio, during which several students were killed by National Guard troops. Protests continued, eventually resulting in the end of the compulsory draft in 1973. In that same year, the US departed Vietnam. In 1975, the South surrendered, and Vietnam became a unified country under communist rule.

## Events of the Gerald Ford Presidency

Gerald Ford was appointed to the vice presidency after Nixon's vice president **Spiro Agnew** resigned in 1973 under charges of tax evasion. With Nixon's resignation, Ford became president.

Ford's presidency saw negotiations with Russia to limit nuclear arms, as well as struggles to deal with inflation, economic downturn, and energy shortages. Ford's policies sought to reduce governmental control of various businesses and reduce the role of government overall. He also worked to prevent escalation of conflicts in the Middle East.

### End of the Cold War and the Dissolution of the Soviet Union

In the late 1980s, **Mikhail Gorbachev** led the Soviet Union. He introduced a series of reform programs. **Ronald Reagan** famously urged Gorbachev to tear down the **Berlin Wall** as a gesture of growing freedom in the Eastern Bloc, and in 1989 it was demolished, ending the separation of East and West Germany. The Soviet Union relinquished its power over the various republics in Eastern Europe, and they became independent nations with their own individual governments. In 1991, the **USSR** was dissolved and the Cold War also came to an end.

**Review Video: How Did the Cold War End?**
Visit mometrix.com/academy and enter code: 278032

### Events of the Jimmy Carter Presidency

Jimmy Carter was elected as president in 1976. Faced with a budget deficit, high unemployment, and continued inflation, Carter also dealt with numerous matters of international diplomacy, including:

- **Torrijos-Carter Treaties**—the US gave control of the Panama Canal to Panama.
- **Camp David Accords**—negotiations between Anwar el-Sadat, the president of Egypt, and Menachem Begin, the Israeli Prime Minister, led to a peace treaty between Egypt and Israel.
- **Strategic Arms Limitation Talks (SALT)**—these led to agreements and treaties between the US and the Soviet Union.
- **Iran Hostage Crisis**—after the Shah of Iran was deposed, an Islamic cleric, Ayatollah Khomeini, came to power. The shah came to the US for medical treatment, and Iran demanded his return so he could stand trial. In retaliation, a group of Iranian students stormed the US Embassy in Iran. Fifty-two American hostages were held for 444 days.

Jimmy Carter was awarded the **Nobel Peace Prize** in 2002.

### Events of the Ronald Reagan Presidency

Ronald Reagan, at 69, became the oldest American president. The two terms of his administration included notable events such as:

- Reaganomics, also known as supply-side, trickle-down, or free-market economics, involving major tax cuts
- Economic Recovery Tax Act of 1981
- First female justice appointed to the Supreme Court—Sandra Day O'Connor
- Massive increase in the national debt—from $1 trillion to $3 trillion
- Reduction of nuclear weapons via negotiations with Mikhail Gorbachev
- Iran-Contra scandal—cover-up of US involvement in revolutions in El Salvador and Nicaragua
- Deregulation of savings and loan industry
- Loss of the space shuttle *Challenger*

## Events of the George H. W. Bush Presidency

Reagan's presidency was followed by a term under his former vice president, **George H. W. Bush**. Bush's run for president included the famous "**thousand points of light**" speech, which was instrumental in increasing his standing in the election polls. During Bush's presidency, numerous international events took place, including:

- Fall of the Berlin wall and Germany's unification
- Panamanian dictator Manuel Noriega captured and tried on drug and racketeering charges
- Dissolution of the Soviet Union
- Gulf War, or Operation Desert Storm, triggered by Iraq's invasion of Kuwait
- Tiananmen Square Massacre in Beijing, China
- Ruby Ridge
- The arrival of the World Wide Web

## Events of the William Clinton Presidency

William Jefferson "Bill" Clinton was the second president in US history to be impeached, but he was not convicted, and maintained high approval ratings in spite of the impeachment. Major events during his presidency included:

- Family and Medical Leave Act
- "Don't Ask, Don't Tell," a compromise position regarding homosexuals serving in the military
- North American Free Trade Agreement, or NAFTA
- Defense of Marriage Act
- Oslo Accords
- Siege at Waco, Texas, involving the Branch Davidians led by David Koresh
- Bombing of the Murrah Federal Building in Oklahoma City, Oklahoma
- Troops sent to Haiti, Bosnia, and Somalia to assist with domestic problems in those areas

## Events of the George W. Bush Presidency

George W. Bush, son of George H. W. Bush, became president after Clinton. Major events during his presidency included:

- September 11, 2001, al-Qaeda terrorists hijack commercial airliners and fly into the World Trade Center towers and the Pentagon, killing nearly 3,000 Americans
- US troops sent to Afghanistan to hunt down al-Qaeda leaders, including the head of the organization, Osama Bin Laden; beginning of the War on Terror
- US troops sent to Iraq, along with a multinational coalition, to depose Saddam Hussein and prevent his deployment of suspected weapons of mass destruction
- Subprime mortgage crisis and near collapse of the financial industry, leading to the Great Recession; first of multiple government bailouts of the financial industry

## Barack Obama

In 2008, Barack Obama, a senator from Illinois, became the first African American US president. His administration focused on improving the lot of a country suffering from a major recession. His major initiatives included:

- Economic bailout packages
- Improvements in women's rights

- Moves to broaden LGBT rights
- Health care reform legislation
- Reinforcement of the war in Afghanistan

## Donald Trump

In 2016, Donald Trump, previously a real estate developer and television personality, was elected 45th president after a tumultuous election in which he won the electoral college but lost the popular vote. Marked by tension between the administration and domestic media, Trump's initiatives included:

- Appointing three Supreme Court Justices: Neil Gorsuch, Brett Kavanaugh, and Amy Coney Barrett
- Passing a major tax reform bill
- Enacting travel and emigration restrictions on eight nations: Iran, Libya, Syria, Yemen, Somalia, Chad, North Korea, and Venezuela
- Recognizing Jerusalem, rather than Tel Aviv, as the capital of Israel
- Responding to the novel coronavirus (SARS-CoV-2) outbreak

Almost completely along party lines, Donald Trump was impeached by the House on charges of abuse of power and obstruction of Congress; he was acquitted by the Senate.

# Geography

## Geography

### GEOGRAPHY

Geography is the study of Earth. Geographers study **physical characteristics** of Earth as well as man-made borders and boundaries. They also study the **distribution of life** on the planet, such as where certain species of animals can be found or how different forms of life interact. Major elements of the study of geography include:

- Locations
- Regional characteristics
- Spatial relations
- Natural and man-made forces that change elements of Earth

These elements are studied from regional, topical, physical, and human perspectives. Geography also focuses on the origins of Earth, as well as the history and backgrounds of different human populations.

### PHYSICAL VS. CULTURAL GEOGRAPHY

Physical geography is the study of the physical characteristics of Earth: how they relate to each other, how they were formed, and how they develop. These characteristics include climate, land, and water, and also how they affect human population in various areas. Different landforms, in combination with various climates and other conditions, determine the characteristics of various cultures.

**Cultural geography** is the study of how the various aspects of physical geography affect individual cultures. Cultural geography also compares various cultures: how their lifestyles and customs are affected by their geographical location, climate, and other factors, as well as how they interact with their environment.

**Review Video: Regional Geography**
Visit mometrix.com/academy and enter code: 350378

### DIVISIONS OF GEOGRAPHICAL STUDY AND TOOLS USED

The four divisions of geographical study and tools used are:

- **Topical**—the study of a single feature of Earth or one specific human activity that occurs worldwide.
- **Physical**—the various physical features of Earth, how they are created, the forces that change them, and how they are related to each other and to various human activities.
- **Regional**—specific characteristics of individual places and regions.
- **Human**—how human activity affects the environment. This includes the study of political, historical, social, and cultural activities.

Tools used in geographical study include special research methods like mapping, field studies, statistics, interviews, mathematics, and the use of various scientific instruments.

## Important Ancient Geographers

The following are three important ancient geographers and their contributions to the study of geography:

- **Eratosthenes** lived in ancient Greek times and mathematically calculated the circumference of Earth and the tilt of Earth's axis. He also created the first map of the world.
- **Strabo** wrote a description of the ancient world called *Geographica* in seventeen volumes.
- **Ptolemy**, primarily an astronomer, was an experienced mapmaker. He wrote a treatise entitled *Geography*, which was used by Christopher Columbus in his travels.

## Ways Geographers Analyze Areas of Human Population

In cities, towns, or other areas where many people have settled, geographers focus on the **distribution** of populations, neighborhoods, industrial areas, transportation, and other elements important to the society in question. For example, they would map out the locations of hospitals, airports, factories, police stations, schools, and housing groups. They would also make note of how these facilities are distributed in relation to the areas of habitation, such as the number of schools in a certain neighborhood or how many grocery stores are located in a specific suburban area. Another area of study and discussion is the distribution of **towns** themselves, from widely spaced rural towns to large cities that merge into each other to form a megalopolis.

## Role of a Cartographer

A cartographer is a mapmaker. Mapmakers produce detailed illustrations of geographic areas to record where various features are located within that area. These illustrations can be compiled into maps, charts, graphs, and even globes. When constructing maps, **cartographers** must take into account the problem of **distortion**. Because Earth is round, a flat map does not accurately represent the correct proportions, especially if a very large geographical area is being depicted. Maps must be designed in such a way as to minimize this distortion and maximize accuracy. Accurately representing Earth's features on a flat surface is achieved through **projection**.

## Types of Projection Used in Creating World Maps

The three major types of projection used in creating world maps are:

- **Cylindrical projection**—this is created by wrapping the globe of Earth in a cylindrical piece of paper, then using a light to project the globe onto the paper. The largest distortion occurs at the outermost edges.
- **Conical projection**—the paper is shaped like a cone and contacts the globe only at the cone's base. This type of projection is most useful for middle latitudes.
- **Flat-Plane projections**—also known as a gnomonic projection, this type of map is projected onto a flat piece of paper that only touches the globe at a single point. Flat-plane projections make it possible to map out Great-Circle routes, or the shortest route between one point and another on the globe, as a straight line.

## Specific Types of Map Projections

Four specific types of map projections that are commonly used today are:

- **Winkel tripel projection**—this is the most common projection used for world maps since it was accepted in 1998 by the National Geographic Society as a standard. The Winkel tripel projection balances size and shape, greatly reducing distortion.
- **Robinson projection**—east and west sections of the map are less distorted, but continental shapes are somewhat inaccurate.

- **Goode homolosine projection**—sizes and shapes are accurate, but distances are not. This projection basically represents a globe that has been cut into connected sections so that it can lie flat.
- **Mercator projection**—though distortion is high, particularly in areas farther from the equator, this cylindrical projection is commonly used by seafarers.

## Major Elements of Any Map

The five major elements of any map are:

- **Title**—this tells basic information about the map, such as the area represented.
- **Legend**—also known as the key, the legend explains what symbols used on a particular map represent, such as symbols for major landmarks.
- **Grid**—this most commonly represents the geographic grid system, or latitude and longitude marks used to precisely locate specific locations.
- **Directions**—a compass rose or other symbol is used to indicate the cardinal directions.
- **Scale**—this shows the relation between a certain distance on the map and the actual distance. For example, one inch might represent one mile, or ten miles, or even more, depending on the size of the map.

**Review Video: 5 Elements of Any Map**
Visit mometrix.com/academy and enter code: 437727

## Equal-Area Maps vs. Conformal Maps

An equal-area map is designed such that the proportional sizes of various areas are accurate. For example, if one landmass is one-fifth the size of another, the lines on the map will be shifted to accommodate for distortion so that the proportional size is accurate. In many maps, areas farther from the equator are greatly distorted; this type of map compensates for this phenomenon. A **conformal map** focuses on representing the correct shape of geographical areas, with less concern for comparative size.

## Consistent Scale Maps and Thematic Maps

With a consistent scale map, the same scale, such as one inch being equal to ten miles, is used throughout the entire map. This is most often used for maps of smaller areas, as maps that cover larger areas, such as the full globe, must make allowances for distortion. Maps of very large areas often make use of more than one scale, with scales closer to the center representing a larger area than those at the edges.

A **thematic map** is constructed to show very specific information about a chosen theme. For example, a thematic map might represent political information, such as how votes were distributed in an election, or could show population distribution or climatic features.

## Relief Maps

A relief map is constructed to show details of various **elevations** across the area of the map. Higher elevations are represented by different colors than lower elevations. **Relief maps** often also show additional details, such as the overall ruggedness or smoothness of an area. Mountains would be represented as ridged and rugged, while deserts would be shown as smooth.

Elevation in relief maps can also be represented by contour lines, or lines that connect points of the same elevation. Some relief maps even feature textures, reconstructing details in a sort of miniature model.

### Geographical Features

- **Mountains** are elevated areas that measure 2,000 feet or more above sea level. Often steep and rugged, they usually occur in groups called chains or ranges. Six of the seven continents on Earth contain at least one range.
- **Hills** are of lower elevation than mountains, at about 500-2,000 feet. Hills are usually more rounded and are found throughout every continent.
- **Plains** are large, flat areas and are usually very fertile. The majority of Earth's population is supported by crops grown on vast plains.
- **Valleys** lie between hills and mountains. Depending on their location, their specific features can vary greatly, from fertile and habitable to rugged and inhospitable.
- **Plateaus** are elevated, but flat on top. Some plateaus are extremely dry, such as the Kenya Plateau, because surrounding mountains prevent them from receiving moisture.
- **Deserts** receive less than ten inches of rain per year. They are usually large areas, such as the Sahara Desert in Africa or the Australian Outback.
- **Deltas** occur at river mouths. Because the rivers carry sediment to the deltas, these areas are often very fertile.
- **Mesas** are flat, steep-sided mountains or hills. The term is sometimes used to refer to plateaus.
- **Basins** are areas of low elevation where rivers drain.
- **Foothills** are the transitional area between plains and mountains, usually consisting of hills that gradually increase in size as they approach a mountain range.
- **Marshes** and **swamps** are also lowlands, but they are very wet and largely covered in vegetation such as reeds and rushes.

### Geographical Terms Referring to Bodies of Water

- The **ocean** refers to the salt water that covers about two-thirds of Earth's surface.
- **Ocean basins** are named portions of the ocean. The five major ocean basins are the Atlantic, Pacific, Indian, Southern, and Arctic.
- **Seas** are generally also salt water, but are smaller than ocean basins and surrounded by land. Examples include the Mediterranean Sea, the Caribbean Sea, and the Caspian Sea.
- **Lakes** are bodies of fresh water found inland. Sixty percent of all lakes are located in Canada.
- **Rivers** are moving bodies of water that flow from higher elevations to lower. They usually start as rivulets or streams and grow until they finally empty into a sea or the ocean.
- **Canals**, such as the Panama Canal and the Suez Canal, are man-made waterways connecting two large bodies of water.

### How Communities Develop

Communities, or groups of people who settle together in a specific area, typically gather where certain conditions exist. These conditions include:

- Easy access to resources such as food, water, and raw materials
- Ability to easily transport raw materials and goods, such as access to a waterway
- Room to house a sufficient workforce

People also tend to form groups with others who are similar to them. In a typical **community**, people can be found who share values, a common language, and common or similar cultural characteristics and religious beliefs. These factors will determine the overall composition of a community as it develops.

### Differences Between Cities in Various Areas of the World

Cities develop and grow as an area develops. Modern statistics show that over half of the world's people live in **cities**. That percentage is even higher in developed areas of the globe. Cities are currently growing more quickly in developing regions, and even established cities continue to experience growth throughout the world. In developing or developed areas, cities often are surrounded by a metropolitan area made up of both urban and suburban sections. In some places, cities have merged into each other and become a **megalopolis**—a single, huge city.

Cities develop differently in different areas of the world. The area available for cities to grow, as well as cultural and economic forces, drives how cities develop. For example, North American cities tend to cover wider areas. European cities tend to have better-developed transportation systems. In Latin America, the richest inhabitants can be found in the city centers, while in North America, wealthier inhabitants tend to live in suburban areas.

In other parts of the world, transportation and communication between cities are less developed. Technological innovations such as the cell phone have increased communication even in these areas. Urban areas must also maintain communication with rural areas in order to procure food, resources, and raw materials that cannot be produced within the city limits.

### Weather vs. Climate

Weather and climate are physical systems that affect geography. Though they deal with similar information, the way this information is measured and compiled is different.

**Weather** involves daily conditions in the atmosphere that affect temperature, precipitation (rain, snow, hail, or sleet), wind speed, air pressure, and other factors. Weather focuses on the short-term—what the conditions will be today, tomorrow, or over the next few days.

In contrast, **climate** aggregates information about daily and seasonal weather conditions in a region over a long period of time. The climate takes into account average monthly and yearly temperatures, average precipitation over long periods of time, and the growing season of an area. Climates are classified according to latitude, or how close they lie to Earth's equator. The three major divisions are:

- **Low Latitudes**, lying from 0 to approximately 23.5 degrees
- **Middle Latitudes**, found from approximately 23.5 to 66.5 degrees
- **High Latitudes**, found from approximately 66.5 degrees to the poles

**Review Video: Climates**
Visit mometrix.com/academy and enter code: 991320

### Climates Found in the Low Latitudes

Rainforests, savannas, and deserts occur in low latitudes:

- **Rainforest** climates, near the equator, experience high average temperatures and humidity, as well as relatively high rainfall.
- **Savannas** are found on either side of the rainforest region. Mostly grasslands, they typically experience dry winters and wet summers.
- Beyond the savannas lie the **desert** regions, with hot, dry climates, sparse rainfall, and temperature fluctuations of up to fifty degrees from day to night.

## Climate Regions Found in the Middle Latitudes

The climate regions found in the middle latitudes are:

- **Mediterranean**—the Mediterranean climate occurs between 30- and 40-degrees latitude, both north and south, on the western coasts of continents. Characteristics include a year-long growing season; hot, dry summers followed by mild winters; and sparse rainfall that occurs mostly during the winter months.
- **Humid-subtropical**—humid-subtropical regions are located in southeastern coastal areas. Winds that blow in over warm ocean currents produce long summers, mild winters, and a long growing season. These areas are highly productive and support a larger part of Earth's population than any other climate.
- **Humid-continental**—the humid continental climate produces the familiar four seasons typical of a good portion of the US. Some of the most productive farmlands in the world lie in these climates. Winters are cold, and summers are hot and humid.

## Marine, Steppe, and Desert Climates

The climate regions found in the middle latitudes are:

- **Marine**—marine climates are found near water or on islands. Ocean winds help make these areas mild and rainy. Summers are cooler than humid-subtropical summers, but winters also bring milder temperatures due to the warmth of the ocean winds.
- **Steppe**—steppe climates, or prairie climates, are found far inland on large continents. Summers are hot and winters are cold, but rainfall is sparser than in continental climates.
- **Desert**—desert climates occur where steppe climates receive even less rainfall. Examples include the Gobi Desert in Asia as well as desert areas of Australia and the southwestern US.

## Climates Found in the High Latitudes

The high latitudes consist of two major climate areas, the tundra and taiga:

- **Tundra** means "marshy plain." The ground is frozen throughout long, cold winters, but there is little snowfall. During the short summers, it becomes wet and marshy. Tundras are not amenable to crops, but many plants and animals have adapted to the conditions.
- **Taigas** lie south of tundra regions and include the largest forest areas in the world, as well as swamps and marshes. Large mineral deposits exist here, as well as many animals valued for their fur. In the winter, taiga regions are colder than the tundra, and summers are hotter. The growing season is short.

A **vertical climate** exists in high mountain ranges. Increasing elevation leads to varying temperatures, growing conditions, types of vegetation and animals, and occurrence of human habitation, often encompassing elements of various other climate regions.

## Factors Affecting Climate

Because Earth is tilted, its **rotation** brings about changes in **seasons**. Regions closer to the equator, and those nearest the poles, experience very little change in seasonal temperatures. Mid-range latitudes are most likely to experience distinct seasons. Large bodies of water also affect climate. Ocean currents and wind patterns can change the climate for an area that lies in a typically cold latitude, such as England, to a much more temperate climate. Mountains can affect both short-term weather and long-term climates. Some deserts occur because precipitation is stopped by the wall of a mountain range.

Over time, established **climate patterns** can shift and change. While the issue is hotly debated, it has been theorized that human activity has also led to climate change.

## Effect of Human Systems

### *Human Systems that Geographers Incorporate into the Study of Earth*

Human systems affect geography in the way in which they settle, form groups that grow into large-scale habitations, and even create permanent changes in the landscape. **Geographers** study movements of people, how they distribute goods among each other and to other settlements or cultures, and how ideas grow and spread. Migrations, wars, forced relocations, and trade can all spread cultural ideas, language, goods, and other practices to widespread areas. Throughout history, cultures have been changed due to a wide range of events, including major migrations and the conquering of one people by another. In addition, **human systems** can lead to various conflicts or alliances to control access to and the use of natural resources.

### *Human Systems that Form the Basis of Cultures in North America*

North America consists of 23 countries, including (in decreasing population order) the United States of America, Mexico, Canada, Guatemala, Cuba, Haiti, and the Dominican Republic. The US and Canada support similarly diverse cultures, as both were formed from groups of native races and large numbers of immigrants. Many **North American cultures** come from a mixture of indigenous and colonial European influences. Agriculture is important to North American countries, while service industries and technology also play a large part in the economy. On average, North America supports a high standard of living and a high level of development and supports trade with countries throughout the world.

### *Human Systems that Shape South America*

Home to twelve sovereign states, including Brazil (largest in area and population), Colombia, Argentina, Venezuela, and Peru; two independent territories; and one internal territory, **South America** is largely defined by its prevailing languages. The majority of countries in South America speak Spanish or Portuguese. Most of South America has experienced a similar history, having been originally dominated by Native cultures and then conquered by European nations. The countries of South America have since gained independence, but there is a wide disparity between various countries' economic and political factors. Most South American countries rely on only one or two exports, usually agricultural, with suitable lands often controlled by rich families. Most societies in South America feature major separations between classes, both economically and socially. Challenges faced by developing South American countries include geographical limitations, economic issues, and sustainable development, including the need to preserve the existing rainforests.

### *Human Systems Influencing Europe*

Europe contains a wide variety of cultures, ethnic groups, physical geographical features, climates, and resources, all of which have influenced the distribution of its varied population. **Europe**, in general, is industrialized and developed, with cultural differences giving each individual country its own unique characteristics. Greek and Roman influences played a major role in European culture, as did Christianity. European countries spread their beliefs and cultural elements throughout the world by means of migration and colonization. They have had a significant influence on nearly every other continent in the world. While Western Europe has been largely democratic, Eastern Europe functioned under communist rule for many years. The formation of the European Union (EU) in 1993 has increased stability and positive diplomatic relations among European nations. Like other industrialized regions, Europe is now focusing on various environmental issues.

### *Human Systems that Have Shaped Russia*

After numerous conflicts, Russia became a Communist state, known as the **USSR**. With the collapse of the USSR in 1991, the country has struggled in its transition to a market-driven economy. Attempts to build a workable system have led to the destruction of natural resources as well as problems with nuclear power, including accidents such as Chernobyl. To complete the transition to a market economy, Russia would need to improve its transportation and communication systems and find a way to more efficiently use its natural resources.

The population of Russia is not distributed evenly, with three-quarters of the population living west of the Ural Mountains. The people of Russia encompass over a hundred different ethnic groups. Over eighty percent of the population is ethnically Russian, and Russian is the official language of the country.

### *Human Systems that Have Shaped North Africa and Southwest and Central Asia*

The largely desert climate of these areas has led most population centers to rise around sources of **water**, such as the Nile River. This area is the home of the **earliest known civilizations** and the origin of Christianity, Judaism, and Islam. After serving as the site of huge, independent civilizations in ancient times, North Africa and Southwest and Central Asia were largely parceled out as **European colonies** during the 18th and 19th centuries. The beginning of the 20th century saw many of these countries gain their independence. **Islam** has served as a unifying force for large portions of these areas, and many of the inhabitants speak Arabic. In spite of the arid climate, agriculture is a large business, but the most valuable resource is **oil**. Centuries of conflict throughout this area have led to ongoing political problems. These political problems have also contributed to environmental issues.

### *Human Systems that Shape and Influence the Culture of Sub-Saharan Africa*

South of the Sahara Desert, **Africa** is divided into a number of culturally diverse nations. The inhabitants are unevenly distributed due to geographical limitations that prevent settlement in vast areas. **AIDS** has become a major plague throughout this part of Africa, killing millions, largely due to restrictive beliefs that prevent education about the disease, as well as abject poverty and unsettled political situations that make it impossible to manage the pandemic. The population of this area of Africa is widely diverse due to extensive **migration**. Many of the people still rely on **subsistence farming** for their welfare. Starvation and poverty are rampant due to drought and political instability. Some areas are far more stable than others due to the greater availability of resources. These areas have been able to begin the process of **industrialization**.

### *Human Systems that Determine the Cultural Makeup of South Asia*

South Asia is home to one of the first human civilizations, which grew up in the **Indus River Valley**. With a great deal of disparity between rural and urban life, South Asia has much to do to improve the quality of life for its lower classes. Two major religions, **Hinduism** and **Buddhism**, have their origins in this region. Parts of South Asia, most notably India, were subject to **British rule** for several decades and are still working to improve independent governments and social systems. Overall, South Asia is very culturally diverse, with a wide mix of religions and languages throughout. Many individuals are **farmers**, but a growing number have found prosperity in the spread of **high-tech industries**. Industrialization is growing in South Asia but continues to face environmental, social, religious, and economic challenges.

### *Human Systems Shaping the Culture of East Asia*

Governments in East Asia are varied, ranging from communist to democratic governments, with some governments that mix both approaches. **Isolationism** throughout the area limited the countries' contact with other nations until the early 20th century. The unevenly distributed population of East Asia consists of over one and a half billion people with widely diverse ethnic backgrounds, religions, and languages. More residents live in **urban** areas than in **rural** areas, creating shortages of farmworkers at times. Japan, Taiwan, and South Korea are overall more urban, while China and Mongolia are more rural. Japan stands as the most industrial country in East Asia. Some areas of East Asia are suffering from major environmental issues. Japan has dealt with many of these problems and now has some of the strictest environmental laws in the world.

### *Human Systems that Have Influenced Southeast Asia*

Much of Southeast Asia was **colonized** by European countries during the 18th and 19th centuries, with the exception of Siam, now known as Thailand. All Southeast Asian countries are now independent, but the 20th century saw numerous conflicts between **communist** and **democratic** forces.

Southeast Asia has been heavily influenced by both Buddhist and Muslim religions. Industrialization is growing, with the population moving in large numbers from rural to urban areas. Some have moved to avoid conflict, oppression, and poverty.

**Natural disasters**, including volcanoes, typhoons, and flash flooding, are fairly common in Southeast Asia, creating extensive economic damage and societal disruption.

### *Human Systems that Affect the Development and Culture of Australia, Oceana, and Antarctica*

**South Pacific** cultures originally migrated from Southeast Asia, creating hunter-gatherer or sometimes settled agricultural communities. **European** countries moved in during later centuries, seeking the plentiful natural resources of the area. Today, some South Pacific islands remain under the control of foreign governments, and culture in these areas mixes modern, industrialized society with indigenous culture. Population is unevenly distributed, largely due to the inhabitability of many parts of the South Pacific, such as the extremely hot desert areas of Australia. **Agriculture** still drives much of the economy, with **tourism** growing. **Antarctica** remains the only continent that has not been claimed by any country. There are no permanent human habitations in Antarctica, but scientists and explorers visit the area on a temporary basis.

## Human-Environment Interaction

Geography also studies the ways people interact with, use, and change their **environment**. The effects, reasons, and consequences of these changes are studied, as are the ways the environment limits or influences human behavior. This kind of study can help determine the best course of action when a nation or group of people is considering making changes to the environment, such as building a dam or removing natural landscape to build or expand roads. Study of the **consequences** can help determine if these actions are manageable and how long-term, detrimental results can be mitigated.

## Physical Geography and Climates

### *Physical Geography and Climate of North America*

Together, the US and Canada make up the majority of North America and both have a similar distribution of geographical features: mountain ranges in both the east and the west, stretches of fertile plains through the center, and lakes and waterways. Both areas were shaped by **glaciers**, which also deposited highly fertile soil. Because they are so large, Canada and the US experience several varieties of **climate**, including continental climates with four seasons in median areas, tropical climates in the southern part of the US, and arctic climes in the far north. The remaining area of North America includes Mexico, Central America, the Caribbean Isles, and Greenland.

### *Physical Geography and Climate of South America*

South America contains a wide variety of geographical features, including high **mountains** such as the Andes, wide **plains**, and high-altitude **plateaus**. The region contains numerous natural resources, but many of them have remained unused due to various obstacles, including political issues, geographic barriers, and lack of sufficient economic power. Climate zones in South America are largely **tropical**, with rainforests and savannas, but vertical climate zones and grasslands also exist in some places.

### *Physical Geography and Climate of Europe*

Europe spans a wide area with a variety of climate zones. In the east and south are **mountain** ranges, while the north is dominated by a **plains** region. The long coastline and the island nature of some countries, such as Britain, mean the climate is often warmer than other lands at similar latitudes, as the area is warmed by **ocean currents**. Many areas of western Europe have a moderate climate, while areas of the south are dominated by the classic Mediterranean climate. Europe carries a high level of natural resources. Numerous waterways help connect the inner regions with the coastal areas. Much of Europe is **industrialized**, and **agriculture** has been developed for thousands of years.

### *Physical Geography and Climate of Russia*

Russia's area encompasses part of Asia and Europe. From the standpoint of square footage alone, **Russia** is the largest country in the world. Due to its size, Russia encompasses a wide variety of climatic regions, including **plains**, **plateaus**, **mountains**, and **tundra**.

Russia's **climate** can be quite harsh, with rivers that are frozen most of the year, making transportation of the country's rich natural resources more difficult. Siberia, in northern Russia, is dominated by **permafrost**. Native peoples in this area still follow a hunting and gathering lifestyle, living in portable yurts and subsisting largely on herds of reindeer or caribou. Other areas include taiga with extensive, dense woods in north-central Russia and more temperate steppes and grasslands in the southwest.

### *Physical Geography and Climate of North Africa, Southwest, and Central Asia*

This area of the world is complex in its geographical structure and climate, incorporating seas, peninsulas, rivers, mountains, and numerous other features. **Earthquakes** are common, with tectonic plates in the area remaining active. Much of the world's **oil** lies in this area. The tendency of the large rivers of North Africa, especially the Nile, to follow a set pattern of **drought** and extreme **fertility**, led people to settle there from prehistoric times. As technology has advanced, people have tamed this river, making its activity more predictable and the land around it more productive. The extremely arid nature of many other parts of this area has also led to **human intervention** such as irrigation to increase agricultural production.

### *Physical Geography and Climate of the Southern Portion of Africa*

South of the Sahara Desert, the high elevations and other geographical characteristics have made it very difficult for human travel or settlement to occur. The geography of the area is dominated by a series of **plateaus**. There are also mountain ranges and a large rift valley in the eastern part of the country. Contrasting the wide desert areas, sub-Saharan Africa contains numerous lakes, rivers, and world-famous waterfalls. The area has **tropical** climates, including rainforests, savannas, steppes, and desert areas. The main natural resources are minerals, including gems and water.

### Physical Geography and Climate of South Asia

The longest **alluvial plain**, a plain caused by shifting floodplains of major rivers and river systems over time, exists in South Asia. South Asia boasts three major **river systems** in the Ganges, Indus, and Brahmaputra. It also has large deposits of **minerals**, including iron ore that is in great demand internationally. South Asia holds mountains, plains, plateaus, and numerous islands. The climates range from tropical to highlands and desert areas. South Asia also experiences monsoon winds that cause a long rainy season. Variations in climate, elevation, and human activity influence agricultural production.

### Geography and Climate of East Asia

East Asia includes North and South Korea, Mongolia, China, Japan, and Taiwan. Mineral resources are plentiful but not evenly distributed throughout. The coastlines are long, and while the population is large, farmlands are sparse. As a result, the surrounding ocean has become a major source of sustenance. East Asia is large enough to encompass several climate regions. **Ocean currents** provide milder climates to coastal areas, while **monsoons** provide the majority of the rainfall for the region. **Typhoons** are somewhat common, as are **earthquakes**, **volcanoes**, and **tsunamis**. The latter occur because of the tectonic plates that meet beneath the continent and remain somewhat active.

### Geography and Climate of Southeast Asia

Southeast Asia lies largely on the **equator**, and roughly half of the countries of the region are island nations. These countries include Indonesia, the Philippines, Vietnam, Thailand, Myanmar, and Malaysia (which is partially on the mainland and partially an island country). The island nations of Southeast Asia feature mountains that are considered part of the **Ring of Fire**, an area where tectonic plates remain active, leading to extensive volcanic activity as well as earthquakes and tsunamis. Southeast Asia boasts many rivers and abundant natural resources, including gems, fossil fuels, and minerals. There are basically two seasons: wet and dry. The wet season arrives with the **monsoons**. In general, Southeast Asia consists of **tropical rainforest climates**, but there are some mountain areas and tropical savannas.

### Geography and Climate of Australia, Oceania, and Antarctica

In the far southern hemisphere of the globe, Australia and Oceania present their own climatic combinations. **Australia**, the only island on Earth that is also a continent, has extensive deserts as well as mountains and lowlands. The economy is driven by agriculture, including ranches and farms, and minerals. While the steppes bordering extremely arid inland areas are suitable for livestock, only the coastal areas receive sufficient rainfall for crops without using irrigation. **Oceania** refers to over 10,000 Pacific islands created by volcanic activity. Most of these have tropical climates with wet and dry seasons. **New Zealand**, Australia's nearest neighbor, boasts rich forests, mountain ranges, and relatively moderate temperatures, including rainfall throughout the year. **Antarctica** is covered with ice. Its major resource consists of scientific information. It supports some wildlife, such as penguins, and little vegetation, primarily mosses or lichens.

## Theory of Plate Tectonics

According to the geological theory of plate tectonics, Earth's crust is made up of ten major and several minor **tectonic plates**. These plates are the solid areas of the crust. They float on top of Earth's mantle, which is made up of molten rock. Because the plates float on this liquid component of Earth's crust, they move, creating major changes in Earth's surface. These changes can happen very slowly over a long time period, such as in continental drift, or rapidly, such as when earthquakes occur. **Interaction** between the different continental plates can create mountain ranges, volcanic activity, major earthquakes, and deep rifts.

### *Types of Plate Boundaries*

*Plate tectonics* defines three types of plate boundaries, determined by how the edges of the plates interact. These **plate boundaries** are:

- **Convergent boundaries**—the bordering plates move toward one another. When they collide directly, this is known as continental collision, which can create very large, high mountain ranges such as the Himalayas and the Andes. If one plate slides under the other, this is called subduction. Subduction can lead to intense volcanic activity. One example is the Ring of Fire that lies along the northern Pacific coastlines.
- **Divergent boundaries**—plates move away from each other. This movement leads to rifts such as the Mid-Atlantic Ridge and East Africa's Great Rift Valley.
- **Transform boundaries**—plate boundaries slide in opposite directions against each other. Intense pressure builds up along transform boundaries as the plates grind along each other's edges, leading to earthquakes. Many major fault lines, including the San Andreas Fault, lie along transform boundaries.

## Erosion, Weathering, Transportation, and Deposition

Erosion involves movement of any loose material on Earth's surface. This can include soil, sand, or rock fragments. These loose fragments can be displaced by natural forces such as wind, water, ice, plant cover, and human factors. **Mechanical erosion** occurs due to natural forces. **Chemical erosion** occurs as a result of human intervention and activities. **Weathering** occurs when atmospheric elements affect Earth's surface. Water, heat, ice, and pressure all lead to weathering. **Transportation** refers to loose material being moved by wind, water, or ice. Glacial movement, for example, carries everything from pebbles to boulders, sometimes over long distances. **Deposition** is the result of transportation. When material is transported, it is eventually deposited, and builds up to create formations like moraines and sand dunes.

## Effects of Human Interaction and Conflict on Geographical Boundaries

Human societies and their interaction have led to divisions of territories into **countries** and various other subdivisions. While these divisions are at their root artificial, they are important to geographers in discussing various populations' interactions.

**Geographical divisions** often occur through conflict between different human populations. The reasons behind these divisions include:

- Control of resources
- Control of important trade routes
- Control of populations

**Conflict** often occurs due to religious, political, language, or race differences. Natural resources are finite and so often lead to conflict over how they are distributed among populations.

## State Sovereignty

State sovereignty recognizes the division of geographical areas into areas controlled by various governments or groups of people. These groups control not only the territory but also all its natural resources and the inhabitants of the area. The entire planet Earth is divided into **political** or **administratively sovereign areas** recognized to be controlled by a particular government, with the exception of the continent of Antarctica.

## Alliances

Alliances form between different countries based on similar interests, political goals, cultural values, or military issues. Six existing **international alliances** include:

- North Atlantic Treaty Organization (NATO)
- Common Market
- European Union (EU)
- United Nations (UN)
- Caribbean Community
- Council of Arab Economic Unity

In addition, very large **companies** and **multi-national corporations** can create alliances and various kinds of competition based on the need to control resources, production, and the overall marketplace.

## Ways Agricultural Revolution Changed Society

The agricultural revolution began approximately 6,000 years ago when the **plow** was invented in **Mesopotamia**. Using a plow drawn by animals, people were able to cultivate crops in large quantities rather than gathering available seeds and grains and planting them by hand. Because large-scale agriculture was labor-intensive, this led to the development of stable communities where people gathered to make farming possible. As **stable farming communities** replaced groups of nomadic hunter-gatherers, human society underwent profound changes. Societies became dependent on limited numbers of crops as well as subject to the vagaries of weather. Trading livestock and surplus agricultural output led to the growth of large-scale **commerce** and **trade routes**.

## Ways Human Populations Modify Their Surrounding Environment

The agricultural revolution led human societies to begin changing their surroundings to accommodate their needs for shelter and room to cultivate food and to provide for domestic animals. Clearing ground for crops, redirecting waterways for irrigation purposes, and building permanent settlements all create major changes in the **environment**. Large-scale agriculture can lead to loose topsoil and damaging erosion. Building large cities leads to degraded air quality, water pollution from energy consumption, and many other side effects that can severely damage the environment. Recently, many countries have taken action by passing laws to **reduce human impact** on the environment and reduce the potentially damaging side effects. This is called **environmental policy**.

## Ecology

Ecology is the study of the way living creatures interact with their environment. **Biogeography** explores the way physical features of Earth affect living creatures.

**Ecology** bases its studies on three different levels of the environment:

- **Ecosystem**—this is a specific physical environment and all the organisms that live there.
- **Biome**—this is a group of ecosystems, usually consisting of a large area with similar flora and fauna as well as similar climate and soil. Examples of biomes include deserts, tropical rain forests, taigas, and tundra.
- **Habitat**—this is an area in which a specific species usually lives. The habitat includes the necessary soil, water, and resources for that particular species, as well as predators and other species that compete for the same resources.

### Types of Interactions Occurring Between Species in an Individual Habitat

Different interactions occur among species and members of single species within a habitat. These **interactions** fall into three categories:

- **Competition** — competition occurs when different animals, either of the same species or of different species, compete for the same resources. Robins can compete with other robins for available food, but other insectivores also compete for these same resources.
- **Predation**— predation occurs when one species depends on the other species for food, such as a fox who subsists on small mammals.
- **Symbiosis** — symbiosis occurs when two different species exist in the same environment without negatively affecting each other. Some symbiotic relationships are beneficial to one or both organisms without harm occurring to either.

### Importance of an Organism's Ability to Adapt

If a species is relocated from one habitat to another, it must **adapt** in order to survive. Some species are more capable of adapting than others. Those that cannot adapt will not survive. There are different ways a creature can adapt, including behavior modification and structural or physiological changes. Adaptation is also vital if an organism's environment changes around it. Although the creature has not been relocated, it finds itself in a new environment that requires changes in order to survive. The more readily an organism can adapt, the more likely it is to survive. The almost infinite ability of **humans** to adapt is a major reason why they are able to survive in almost any habitat in any area of the world.

### Biodiversity

Biodiversity refers to the variety of habitats that exist on the planet, as well as the variety of organisms that can exist within these habitats. A greater level of **biodiversity** makes it more likely that an individual habitat will flourish along with the species that depend upon it. Changes in habitat, including climate change, human intervention, or other factors, can reduce biodiversity by causing the extinction of certain species.

# Practice Test #1

**1. Which of the following aspects of civilization were first developed as early as 5,000 years ago?**

a. Centralized governments
b. The Dialogues of Socrates
c. Building of the Parthenon
d. The recording of the Torah

**2. When did the "Father of Medicine," after whom today's oath "First do no harm" live?**

a. After the development of Euclidean geometry
b. Before Archimedes's famous bathtub discovery
c. When Mexico's Temple of the Sun was erected
d. After Aristotle's completed his Western philosophy

**3. Which of the following events in ancient history occurred earliest in time?**

a. The suicide of Cleopatra, the last Pharaoh of Egypt
b. The assassination of Roman Emperor, Julius Caesar
c. The revolt of the Maccabees of Israel against Seleucids
d. The slaves' rebellion against Rome led by Spartacus

**4. Which of the following events affecting the Roman Empire and Christianity came latest?**

a. Widespread Roman persecution of Christians first began
b. Gothic and Frankish tribes escalated invasions in Europe
c. Emperor Constantine the Great passed the Edict of Milan
d. The Council of Nicaea defined Orthodox Christian beliefs

**5. Among these actions by European ancestor tribes contributing to the fall of the Roman Empire, which one took place last?**

a. The Visigoth King Alaric I sacked the city of Rome
b. Mongol Attila the Hun invaded Roman provinces
c. The tribe known as the Vandals destroyed Rome
d. Ostrogoths Theodoric founded his Kingdom of Italy

**6. How long did the period known as the Middle Ages, in Europe, last?**

a. 100 years
b. 500 years
c. 1,000 years
d. 1,200 years

**7. Who was most responsible for the development of medieval universities in the 11th century?**

a. King Charlemagne
b. Pope Gregory VII
c. Robert Sorbon
d. John Balliol

**8. Which of the following did China's Han Dynasty and Europe's Western Roman Empire share in common?**

a. Both suffered population loss from plagues
b. Both reigned for roughly the same duration
c. Both were succeeded by stronger empires
d. Both fell without the influence of income taxes

**9. Which statement is true about medieval Byzantium?**

a. It endured 11 centuries after Constantinople's founding
b. It was primarily Muslim in its religion until the 7th century
c. It was highly unstable in character during medieval times
d. Its strongest times were noted for intellectual advances

**10. Which statement most accurately describes the relationship of medieval Byzantium to the Renaissance in Europe?**

a. Medieval Byzantium delayed the advent of the European Renaissance
b. Medieval Byzantium prepared the way for the European Renaissance
c. Medieval Byzantium had no relationship to the European Renaissance
d. Medieval Byzantium's unity opposed the diversity of the Renaissance

**11. What was true about the Eastern and Western versions of early Christianity?**

a. The government of the Roman Empire did not recognize Christianity in the 5th century
b. Eastern and Western Europe's Christianity were essentially the same in the 4th century
c. The Western Christian Church had a centralized leadership; the Eastern Church did not
d. Regardless of locations, members of the Eastern and Western Churches all spoke Latin

**12. Which of the following is true of the Great Schism?**

a. It occurred in European churches during the 10th century AD.
b. It was the separation of the Protestants from the Catholics
c. It established separation of Christians from non-Christians
d. It created Roman Catholic and Eastern Orthodox Churches

**13. Which of the following factors contributing to the change from the Medieval to Renaissance period in the Western world occurred first in time?**

a. Gutenberg's invention of the movable type printing press
b. The end to the Hundred Years' War of England and France
c. The fall of Constantinople and Byzantium to the Ottomans
d. Christopher Columbus's visit to the New World of Americas

**14. Which is a true statement about how the Middle Ages gave way to the Renaissance?**

a. The change in periods was quite abrupt in historical terms
b. The same events led to this change across various nations
c. The change in the periods was actually a gradual transition
d. The change relates to various time periods among nations

**15. After the fall of the Han Dynasty, which dynasty was next to reunite North and South China?**

a. The Tang Dynasty
b. The Song Dynasty
c. The Sui Dynasty
d. No dynasty

**16. What is true about the golden age in China between the 7th and 13th centuries C.E.?**

a. The Chinese had no knowledge of movable type until the 15th century when Gutenberg invented the printing press in Germany
b. The Chinese were not involved with algebra, which was developed by the Arabs; they learned it from them without changes
c. The years during this golden age brought great prosperity and power to China, while its population remained stable
d. The Chinese achieved the innovation of manufacturing gunpowder during this golden age, enabling explosive weaponry

**17. Which of the following is accurate about China's golden age between 618 and 1279 C.E.?**

a. Toward the end of this age, China strengthened the Silk Road trade routes
b. Importing Vietnamese rice enabled annual harvests to double in this period
c. The later Song Dynasty ruled a larger part of China than the Han or Tang did
d. This period included religious development but not mutual religion exchange

**18. Of the following, which Renaissance figure was best known as a fine artist and painter?**

a. Dante
b. Petrarch
c. Masaccio
d. Gutenberg

**19. Which Italian Renaissance figure was best known as a political philosopher?**

a. Dante Alighieri
b. Leonardo Da Vinci
c. Francesco Petrarca
d. Niccolò Machiavelli

**20. Which of the following was first to write a work in vernacular Italian rather than Latin?**

a. Dante Alighieri
b. Niccolò Machiavelli
c. Francesco Petrarca
d. Pico della Mirandola

**21. In Western Europe, which ancient Greek's works would most likely have been studied by scholars before the Renaissance in the Middle Ages?**

a. Homer
b. Sophocles
c. Thucydides
d. Archimedes

**22. What is true about Martin Luther's 95 Theses?**

a. Luther was opposed to the Church's sales of indulgences
b. Luther believed in practicing simony to support churches
c. Luther felt that clerical celibacy should be better enforced
d. Luther supported the majority of the church's sacraments

**23. Which of the following is correct relative to the Protestant Reformation in Europe?**

a. The end of the Thirty Years' War triggered the Protestant Reformation
b. The Protestant work ethic was credited with capitalism and prosperity
c. The Treaty of Westphalia impeded the development of Protestantism
d. The Treaty of Westphalia reinforced the political authority of the Pope

**24. Of the following, whose ancient civilization was found in what is now Peru?**

a. The Mayans
b. The Aztecs
c. The Incas
d. All of these

**25. Which of these ancient American civilizations was NOT known to have a written language?**

a. All of these
b. The Mayans
c. The Aztecs
d. The Incas

*Questions 26 – 27 pertain to the following Table 2:*

**Population of Detroit, 1950 to 2000**

| Year | 1950 | 1960 | 1970 | 1980 | 1990 | 2000 |
|---|---|---|---|---|---|---|
| Population (in millions) | 1.84 | 1.67 | 1.51 | 1.20 | 1.03 | 0.90 |

**26. The population decline illustrated in Table 2 can be attributed mainly to which of the following factors?**

a. The decline of Detroit's major industry, car manufacturing
b. A decline in the steel industry in cities neighboring Detroit
c. High municipal taxes in Detroit
d. None of the above

**27. The information in Table 2 could be more effectively presented in which of the following formats?**

a. A stem and leaf plot
b. A boxplot
c. A line graph
d. A pie graph

*Questions 28 - 29 pertain to the following Table 3:*

**Population and Population Growth Rates for Four Countries**

| Country | Estimated Population (2011) | Estimated Annual Population Growth |
|---|---|---|
| **Russia** | 142,905,200 | –0.51% |
| **China** | 1,339,724,852 | 0.48% |
| **United States** | 311,417,000 | 0.97% |
| **Vietnam** | 87,375,000 | 1.32% |

**28. According to the information in Table 3, which of the following is most likely to be true of Russia's population at the end of 2016?**

a. It will be less than 1 million
b. It will be over 1 billion
c. It will be less than 142,900,000
d. It will be over 150,000,000

**29. According to the information in Table 3, which of the following countries has the highest estimated annual population growth?**

a. Russia
b. China
c. United States
d. Vietnam

**30. The United States receives the majority of its immigration from Mexico and other Latin American countries, while Western Europe receives a large share of its immigration from Africa. This information supports which of the following arguments?**

a. Immigrants typically move to countries that are more economically prosperous than their own
b. Immigrants typically move to countries that are geographically proximate to their own
c. Both A and B
d. None of the above

**31. Which of the following is an example of a refugee?**

a. A Chinese student who comes to the United States to study engineering and then returns to her home country
b. An illegal immigrant who comes to the United States to work and sends money home to her family
c. An African immigrant who comes to the United States to escape political persecution in his home country
d. A Middle Eastern student who comes to the United States to earn his medical degree and eventually becomes a naturalized American citizen

**32. The United States experienced a "baby boom" in the years immediately following the end of World War II. Which of the following statements best summarizes this event?**

a. It was an increase in fertility rates that resulted from the return of soldiers from war and the post-WWII economic boom
b. Following WWII, it became more socially acceptable for women to bear children out of wedlock, and so the number of single mothers dramatically increased
c. The end of WWII saw a massive increase in immigration, and these immigrants tended to have very high fertility rates
d. The introduction of social welfare into the United States encouraged families to bear more children, even if they could not afford to care for them

**33. Population growth in the American Southwest differs from population growth in other parts of the United States in which of the following ways?**

a. It endangers native plants and animals
b. It causes air and water pollution
c. It is endangered by limited water resources
d. It is endangered by lack of physical infrastructure

**34. After a tsunami devastated Southeast Asia, international authorities moved to put an early warning system in place in order to mitigate the number of casualties caused by future tsunamis. This is PRIMARILY an example of which of the following?**

a. Humans modifying the natural environment to suit their needs
b. Humans adapting to hazards within their natural environment
c. Humans remaining dependent on their natural environment
d. Human activity harming the natural environment

**35. El Niño is a climate pattern that is characterized by higher surface temperatures and higher air surface pressure in the western Pacific Ocean that occurs approximately every five years. This weather pattern is known for having which of the following impacts on human activity?**

a. Droughts in some regions lead to fires and crop failures
b. Increased hurricane activity damages property and endangers lives
c. Unusually cold, snowy winters in North America cause dangerous driving conditions and strand people in their homes
d. All of the above

**36. In urban areas that experience severe flooding, which of the following is the most pressing environmental concern?**

a. Death of certain tree species due to suffocation
b. Contamination of drinking water supplies
c. Loss of crops
d. Reduction in tourism

**37. Large-scale migration from a rural area in which subsistence agriculture is the main way of life to a similar, neighboring area is MOST likely to be caused by which of the following factors?**

a. Low crop prices have caused economic hardship and forced people off of their land
b. A drought has caused food shortages and famine is taking hold
c. The neighboring rural area has better schools, health care, and sanitation facilities
d. A conflict is in progress between the inhabitants of the two rural areas

**38. Biomes are regions defined by which of the following?**

a. Climate
b. Population density
c. Language
d. Political boundaries

**39. Which of the following statements is true of cultural regions?**

a. They typically align with national boundaries
b. They are defined primarily by shared religion
c. They cannot overlap one another
d. They vary greatly in size and scope

**40. In order to be characterized as a functional cultural region, an area must have which of the following?**

a. A common language
b. A common religion
c. A central organizational structure
d. A shared sense of community

**41. The physical locations of Native American cultural regions in the present-day United States, such as those in northeastern Arizona and eastern Oklahoma, are determined PRIMARILY by which of the following factors?**

a. The location of Native American tribes' traditional homelands
b. The suitability of land to Native American tribes' traditional agricultural practices
c. The legally designated locations of Native American tribes' reservations
d. The locations' proximity to protected natural areas

**42. Negative cultural stereotypes may be based on which of the following?**

a. Negative portrayals of members of a certain culture in the media
b. Negative experiences with individual members of a certain culture
c. Fear of members of a certain culture due to threatening acts by a few members of that culture
d. All of the above

**43. For every 1,000 live births in Guatemala, approximately 27 children die before the age of 5. In contrast, the United States has only about 6 deaths per 1,000 live births, and Singapore has only about 2 deaths per every 1,000 live births. This information supports which of the following inferences about life in Guatemala?**

a. There are fewer children born overall in Guatemala than in the United States or Singapore
b. Guatemala's rate of infant mortality is higher than the world average
c. Health care and nutrition for children in Guatemala are poorer than they are in the United States and Singapore
d. Most of the deaths of Guatemalan children under the age of five are caused by malaria

**44. In Bangladesh, only about 44 percent of adults age 15 and older have achieved basic literacy. In contrast, approximately 99 percent of Japanese adults age 15 and older can read. Based on this information, which of the following statements is MOST likely to be true of life in Bangladesh?**

a. Three-quarters of Bangladeshis work in the business and information sectors
b. Most Bangladeshis have never attended school at all
c. Most working-age Bangladeshis are unemployed
d. Many Bangladeshis live in poverty

**45. Languages are divided into families, and each language in a family shares its historical origins with the others in its family. Which of the following languages is NOT part of the same family as the others?**

a. English
b. French
c. Portuguese
d. Chinese

**46. In which of the following countries is the majority of the population NOT Catholic?**

a. Mexico
b. Russia
c. Spain
d. Ireland

**47. Which of the following is a factor that severely restricts women's economic opportunities in some countries?**

a. Laws that prohibit divorce
b. Wide availability of microfinance
c. Laws that guarantee a quota of legislative seats to women
d. Laws that prevent women from owning property

**48. The growth of trade between India and Britain during the colonial era had which of the following cultural effects in Britain?**

a. Slavery became common practice in Britain
b. British citizens adopted the Indian style of dress
c. Products from India, such as tea, became everyday staples in Britain
d. British citizens began to adopt Indian religious practices on a large scale

**49. Which of the following statements describes a major effect that the introduction of television had on American political culture during the mid-1900s?**

a. It allowed citizens to see political events like speeches, revolutions, and wars play out firsthand
b. It provided a public forum where Americans could debate policies
c. It introduced programming that challenged the social mores of the time
d. It provided a new forum for the education of children

**50. Traditional eating patterns in the developing countries of Asia have eroded due MAINLY to which of the following changes?**

a. The introduction of convenient and low-priced prepackaged and fast-food products
b. Higher educational attainment and smaller families
c. Lack of access to traditional food ingredients
d. Failure to teach traditional food ways to children

# Answer Key and Explanations

**1. A:** The first centralized governments were developed concurrently and independently by the ancient river valley civilizations about 5,000 years ago, that is, from around 3000 to 2000 BC. These societies included the Egyptian, Nubian, and Mesopotamian civilizations in the Middle East; the Harappan civilization in India; and China's Yellow River valley civilizations. In ancient Greece, Plato recorded Socrates's Dialogues between 400 and 300 BC, and the Parthenon was built around the 400s BC. The earliest dating from conservative scholars would date the Torah, or the first five books of the Hebrew bible, from around 1400 to 1200 BC. Most critical biblical scholars employing the documentary hypothesis would date sections of the Torah much later anywhere from 950 to 600 BC with its completion around 500 to 400 BC.

**2. B:** Ancient Greek physician Hippocrates, known as the "Father of Medicine" and after whom the Hippocratic Oath still used today was named, lived circa 460 to 370 BC before mathematician Euclid developed his system of geometry and also before scientist Archimedes discovered the principle of displacement of water by solid objects while taking a bath, both in the 200s BC. The Temple of the Sun was constructed at Teotihuacán, Mexico, circa 300 BC, after Hippocrates's death. Ancient Greek philosopher Aristotle (384–322 BC), first to produce a comprehensive Western philosophical system, produced the bulk of his work between 335 and 323 BC, after Hippocrates's lifetime.

**3. C:** The Jewish rebel army of the Maccabees staged an uprising against the Seleucid Empire in 167 BC. This rebellion was notable as the Maccabees reestablished Jewish control of Judea, reaffirmed the Jewish religion, extended Israel's boundaries, and founded the Hasmonean Dynasty (164–63 BC), which some historians believe set the Jewish Biblical canon. A number of rebellions against the Roman Republic were made by its slaves, the most notable one led by the slave Spartacus in 71 BC Roman Emperor Julius Caesar, instrumental in turning the Roman Republic into the Roman Empire, was assassinated as a dictator through a conspiracy by a group of his senators in 44 BC. Cleopatra ruled Egypt from 51 BC until her 30 BC suicide.

**4. D:** The Council of Nicaea first outlined the doctrines of Orthodox Christianity in 325 AD. This occurred after Emperor Constantine the Great issued the Edict of Milan legalizing Christianity in 313. The increasing invasions of Gothic and Frankish tribes in Europe took place in the second half of the 3rd century AD, that is, circa 250–300. Roughly 30 years after the Romans crucified Jesus Christ, they initiated more widespread persecution of Christians in 64 AD. (This persecution intensified even more in the 200s, but the tribal invasions combined with inadequate leadership undermined the Western Roman Empire, contributing to the fall of the Roman Empire and allowing Christianity to spread in the absence of Rome's unifying power.)

**5. D:** The foundation of the Kingdom of Italy by Visigoth (East German tribal ancestor) Theodoric the Great took place in 493 AD. King Alaric I had previously sacked the city of Rome in the year 410 AD, the first time Rome had fallen to an enemy in 800 years. In 433 AD., Attila the Hun, a chieftain of the Mongol tribes from central Asia, attacked a number of provinces that Rome had ruled. The Vandals, an Eastern Germanic tribe, destroyed the city of Rome in 455 AD. Theodoric established the Kingdom of Italy 38 years later.

**6. C:** In Europe, the Middle Ages, or Medieval period, lasted from approximately 500 to 1500 AD. It began with the fall of the Western Roman Empire and ended with the beginning of the Renaissance (meaning rebirth), when interest in knowledge and culture were reawakened, including a revival of the ancient Greek and Roman influences from before the Middle Ages.

**7. B:** In 1079, Pope Gregory VII issued a papal decree that mandated the establishment of cathedral schools to educate the clergy. This resulted in multiple educational centers, which eventually developed into medieval universities. Charlemagne, the King of the Carolingian Empire, reigned earlier, during the 9th century. He was responsible for decreeing the creation of the earlier cathedral schools to educate boys to become clerical bureaucrats for the administration of the Empire. Robert Sorbon sponsored a theological college in Paris, France, later than Pope Gregory's 1079 decree, in 1231; it developed over centuries into Sorbonne University. John Balliol founded one of the earliest colleges, Balliol College in Oxford, England, in 1260.

**8. A:** In both the Han Dynasty of China and the Western Roman Empire of Europe, the populations were reduced by epidemics of plagues. Both did not reign for the same duration: The Han Dynasty lasted around 200 years, while the Western Roman Empire lasted around 900 years. Both were not succeeded by stronger empires; both empires fell not to stronger rulers or regimes but to multiple damages, including the plagues, low birth rates, conflicts and political corruption from within, and barbarian tribes' invasions from without. An additional factor was the influence of income taxes: Both empires failed to collect sufficient tax monies to support their governments.

**9. A:** It is true that, in the Medieval period, Byzantium continued for 1,100 years beyond the foundation of the capital of Constantinople in 330 AD. Byzantium was the name for the Christian part of the Eastern Roman Empire. Hence, it was primarily Christian in religion until the 7th century, preserving Mediterranean Roman culture until Islam began to develop in Eastern Europe. Medieval Byzantium was not unstable but was the most stable European state during those times. Byzantium's strongest times were noted not for intellectual advances but for religious development.

**10. B:** The Eastern European state of Byzantium in the Middle Ages helped to prepare the way for the emergence of the Renaissance in Europe through Byzantine ethnic diversity, stability, cultural strength, its central location, world prominence, urban centers comprising a network, and multiple cultural influences. These factors encouraged rather than delayed the Renaissance. Byzantium was unified and stable but not antithetical to coming Renaissance diversity; Byzantium too was characterized by diversity, among the ethnicity of its populations and cultural influences from Greek, Roman, and Oriental civilizations.

**11. C:** In the early days of Christianity in Europe, the Western Christian Church was governed by one bishop situated in Rome. However, the Eastern Christian Church was governed by multiple bishops at locations including Antioch, Jerusalem, Alexandria, and Constantinople. The government of the Roman Empire did recognize Christianity and by the 4th, not 5th, century: Emperor Constantine the Great legalized Christianity in 313 AD through the Edict of Milan. In fact, by the 5th century, Christianity was the only religion recognized by Roman government. Even in the 4th century, though, Eastern and Western Europe's Christianity differed, not only politically but also socially, culturally, and linguistically: The Western Church spoke Latin, but the Eastern Church spoke Greek.

**12. D:** The Great Schism permanently divided the Catholic Church into the Roman Catholic Church in Western Europe and the Eastern Orthodox Church in Eastern Europe. This occurred during the 11th century AD and not the 10th. It did not involve Protestants, who did not emerge until the 16th century with the Protestant Reformation spearheaded by Martin Luther. It did not separate Christianity from other religions but was an internal splitting of the Catholic Church.

**13. A:** Gutenberg invented the movable-type printing press in 1445. This replaced handwriting for the mass production of books, enabling a shift from medieval public illiteracy to mass literacy that contributed to the Renaissance explosion of revived interest in education and culture. The Hundred Years' War between England and France ended in 1453. Consequently, England moved from continental power to naval strength; and the nations of Europe began to develop modern militaries and political states. Also in 1453, the Ottomans took Constantinople, signaling the end of the Byzantine Empire and beginning of the Ottoman Empire in Eastern Europe. Columbus landed in Central America in 1492 and subsequently explored the Americas, marking the start of European colonial expansion abroad.

**14. C:** The change from the Medieval to the Renaissance time period did not occur suddenly but happened through a gradual transitional process. This transition was stimulated by different events in different nations. It also occurred during different time periods within the longer timeline in different countries. Because of these factors, historians rightly avoid assigning specific dates or events to the end of the Middle Ages and the beginning of the Renaissance.

**15. B:** The Song Dynasty reunited North and South China. China's Han Dynasty fell in 220 AD. There followed many local dynasties for 350 years, but none was able to reunite China. In 589 AD, the Emperor Wendi achieved reunification of the Northern and Southern parts of the country with the Sui Dynasty. During the Sui years, the Grand Canal was built and the Great Wall of China rebuilt. However, despite these achievements, peasants rebelled against the associated labor and taxation, overthrowing the Sui by 618. It was succeeded by the Tang Dynasty, which reigned from 618 to 907. At the end of the Tang, China was decentralized until 960, when General Taizu reunited it, becoming the first emperor of the Song Dynasty.

**16. D:** One of many innovations during China's golden age from 618 to 1279 under the Tang and Song Dynasties was the development of gunpowder, an advance benefiting the military by allowing explosives manufacture. Although Gutenberg invented Europe's first movable-type printing press in 1445 in Renaissance Germany, the Chinese also invented movable-type printing earlier in their country during this golden age, while Europe was still in the Middle Ages, isolated without the Roman Empire's previous knowledge, culture, and trade connections, so this Chinese innovation did not spread to Europe then. The Arabs did develop algebra; however, the Chinese also added innovations to both algebra and arithmetic, including negative numbers, during this golden age. This period brought not only wealth and power; China's population also doubled.

**17. B:** During China's golden age between the 7th and 13th centuries C.E., an agricultural innovation was its importation of a strain of Vietnamese rice that ripened faster, enabling farmers to reap double the annual crops to feed the rapidly growing populations of China's cities. While earlier in the Tang Dynasty, its imperial guards protected the east–west trade routes of the Silk Roads, later on as the dynasty gradually declined, it lost control of these overland routes. The Chinese invention of the magnetic compass helped them transition to maritime trading. The Song Dynasty actually ruled a smaller empire than the Han or Tang Dynasty. However, the Song did perpetuate the power, wealth, and stability of China established during the Tang period. China's golden age did include mutual exchange of religions: Vietnam, Korea, and Japan learned of Buddhism from China, while Eastern Orthodox Christianity and Islam were introduced to China through trade with Europe and the Middle East.

**18. C:** Masaccio was an Italian fine artist and painter of the Renaissance. He was known for being the first to use linear perspective and the vanishing point in his paintings. He also used chiaroscuro (a technique of contrasting light and dark). His paintings were innovative for being more realistic, three-dimensional, and lifelike. Dante (Alighieri), also Italian, was a writer most famous for his

Divine Comedy as well as La Vita Nuova (The New Life) and other works. Petrarch was another Italian and was a great lyrical poet of the Renaissance. Gutenberg, a German, was famous for inventing a movable-type printing press during the Renaissance.

**19. D:** Niccolò Machiavelli, perhaps best known for his book The Prince, was an Italian Renaissance political philosopher noted for writing more realistic representations and rational interpretations of politics. In The Prince, he popularized the political concept of "the ends justify the means." Dante Alighieri was a great poet famous for his Commedia (additionally labeled Divina by contemporary poet and author Boccaccio, who wrote the Decameron and other works) or Divine Comedy, a trilogy consisting of Inferno, Purgatorio, and Paradiso (Hell, Purgatory, and Heaven). Dante's work helped propel the transition from the Medieval period to the Renaissance. Francesco Petrarca, known in English as Petrarch, was famous for his lyrical poetry, particularly sonnets.

**20. A:** Dante Alighieri wrote his Divine Comedy, the first major literary work known to be written in Italian, between 1308 and 1321. In the Medieval period, the masses were illiterate, and the only reading and writing was done by religious scholars in Latin, the language of the Roman Empire. Vernacular languages subsequently developed in Europe when Latin mixed with local languages and evolved into Italian, French, Spanish, and so on. Machiavelli wrote his most famous book, Il Principe (The Prince), and other works in Italian but in the 16th century, 200 years after Dante. Francesco Petrarca, or Petrarch, lived and wrote in the 14th century. He wrote some poetry in Italian, but as a scholar and fan of Latin, he wrote other poetry and many other works mostly in Latin. Pico della Mirandola, a Renaissance humanist famous for his 1486 oration De Hominis Dignitate (On the Dignity of Man), wrote this and his other works in Latin.

**21. D:** Archimedes was an ancient Greek physicist, mathematician, astronomer, engineer, and inventor. He made many innovations, especially in physics. During the Middle Ages, Western European scholars did study ancient Greek texts but only those pertaining to mathematics, the sciences, and philosophy and theology. They did not study ancient Greek works of poetry, drama, oratory, or history. Homer was an ancient Greek poet, Sophocles an ancient Greek dramatist, and Thucydides an ancient Greek historian. Until the Renaissance, only Byzantine scholars in Eastern Europe studied these works.

**22. A:** Among his 95 Theses, which set off the Protestant Reformation, Martin Luther placed major emphasis on his opposition to the Catholic Church's practice of selling indulgences (cancellations of temporal punishment for forgiven sins). He cited simony—that is, buying and selling clerical positions—as well as the sale of indulgences as evidence of the Church's systemic corruption. Another Catholic practice Luther disagreed with was the celibacy of clerics, including monasticism. In addition, Luther and other Protestant reformers objected to most of the Catholic Church's seven sacraments.

**23. B:** The emphasis of the Protestant Reformers on the virtues of hard work has been credited with contributing to the development of modern capitalism and its success in improving the economies of those practicing it. The Protestant Reformation (Martin Luther posted his 95 Theses in 1517) triggered a series of many religious wars between opposing camps, which came to a head in the Thirty Years' War (1618–1648). The Treaty of Westphalia (1648) not only ended this war; it also eliminated the Pope's political authority and gave states the right to choose their religious denominations, thereby facilitating the further development of Protestantism.

**24. C:** The ancient civilization of the Incas was located in what is today the South American country of Peru. The ancient civilization of the Mayans lived in the south of Mexico, on the Yucatan peninsula, and in parts of Central America. The ancient civilization of the Aztecs lived in what is Mexico today.

**25. D:** The Incas, as far as historians know, did NOT commit their spoken language to a written symbol system. (Note that some historians believe that strings the Incas knotted, called Quipu, may have equated to a writing system, though this has not been verified.) The Mayans were known for developing the most comprehensive, authentic written language of the Pre-Columbian Native American societies. A play written in Achi, one of the Mayan languages, has been deemed a masterpiece by the United Nations Educational, Scientific and Cultural Organization (UNESCO). The Aztecs' written language was Nàhuatl.

**26. A:** The population decline illustrated in Table 2 can be attributed mainly to the decline of Detroit's major industry, car manufacturing. As the number of jobs available in Detroit declined, it experienced negative net migration, with more people moving out than moving in.

**27. C:** The information in Table 2 could be more effectively presented in a line graph. This is true because the data show a steady decline over time, and line graphs are most appropriate for showing change over time. Pie graphs are designed to show data about a specific point in time.

**28. C:** It is most likely that Russia's population will be less than 142,900,000 in 2016. Since the population is declining at a rate of about –0.51 percent per year, it will probably decline by about 73,000 people per year. This means that in 2016, Russia's population is likely to be less than 142,900,000, but certainly not less than 1 million.

**29. D:** According to the table, Vietnam has the highest estimated annual population growth, at 1.32 percent per year. The United States has the second highest population growth rate. It is estimated to be about 0.97 percent per year.

**30. C:** This information supports both the argument that immigrants typically move to countries that are more economically prosperous than their own and that immigrants typically move to countries that are geographically proximate to their own. Since many immigrants are seeking out economic opportunity, they tend to immigrate to wealthier countries. Since their means are often limited, they are also more likely to immigrate to countries that are closer and therefore less expensive and less difficult to reach.

**31. C:** An African immigrant who comes to the United States to escape political persecution in his home country is an example of a refugee. A refugee is an individual who leaves his or her home country to escape political, social, or religious persecution.

**32. A:** The post-WWII "baby boom" is best described as an increase in fertility rates resulting from the return of soldiers from war and the post-WWII economic boom. There was also a smaller "echo" baby boom in the 1980s and early 1990s, as the baby boomers' children reached childbearing age.

**33. C:** Population growth in the American Southwest differs from population growth in other parts of the United States because it is endangered by limited water resources. Cities in the arid American Southwest like Las Vegas, Phoenix, and Los Angeles must carefully plan their growth while considering the limited water resources that are available in this part of the United States. While population growth throughout the United States can threaten native species and cause pollution, the lack of water resources is unique to the Southwest.

**34. B:** This scenario is primarily an example of humans adapting to hazards within their natural environment. Since the causes of tsunamis are beyond humans' ability to manipulate, citizens of areas threatened by tsunamis have adapted to their natural environment by implementing measures to mitigate the hazard posed by tsunamis. Similarly, citizens in earthquake-prone areas cannot prevent earthquakes, so they mitigate the hazard posed by earthquakes by building quake-resistant structures.

**35. A:** El Niño is a weather pattern that is known for causing droughts in some regions that lead to fires and crop failures. This effect is most pronounced in certain parts of Africa, Asia, and Australia. El Niño typically suppresses hurricane activity, and it produces unusually mild winters in most parts of North America.

**36. B:** Contamination of drinking water supplies is the most pressing environmental concern in urban areas that experience severe flooding. Drinking water and other standing water can become contaminated with untreated sewage, which in turn taints drinking water supplies and creates the risk of waterborne disease spreading among the population. Loss of crops and trees is less problematic in urban areas, and loss of tourist revenue is an economic, not an environmental, problem.

**37. B:** Large-scale migration from a rural area in which subsistence agriculture is the main way of life to a similar, neighboring area is most likely to be caused by a drought and subsequent famine. Since both areas revolve around subsistence agriculture, it is highly likely that they share similar levels of economic development, and offer only minimal health, education, and sanitation infrastructure. Thus, economic migration between the two areas is unlikely. If there were a conflict between the two regions, this would also be unlikely to result in the situation described.

**38. A:** Biomes are regions defined primarily by climate. They are also called ecosystems, and are typically characterized by similar soils, organisms, and levels of precipitation. They may be either land based or aquatic.

**39. D:** It is true that cultural regions vary greatly in size and scope. Although they sometimes align with national boundaries, this is not always the case. Cultural regions can cover multiple countries, and they can also cover small areas within countries. A cultural region is defined as an area in which most inhabitants share one or more cultural traits, such as language, religion, architecture, cuisine, dress, or social customs. In some cultural regions, inhabitants will share most of these traits, while inhabitants of larger cultural regions will share only one trait.

**40. C:** In order to be characterized as a functional cultural region, an area must have a central node and organizational structure, as well as defined borders. Its inhabitants need not share any cultural traits, such as language or religion, and they do not necessarily have a common sense of community, as is necessary for a perceptual region.

**41. C:** The physical locations of Native American cultural regions in the present-day United States, such as those in northeastern Arizona and eastern Oklahoma, are determined primarily by the legally designated location of Native American tribes' reservations. With the exception of Alaska Natives, who were not removed from their lands and thus do not live on reservations, most Native American tribes were forced from their traditional homelands onto reservations, so current Native American cultural areas are based around these reservations.

**42. D:** Negative cultural stereotypes may be based on a variety of factors, including negative portrayals of members of a certain culture in the media, negative experiences with individual members of a certain culture, and fear of members of a certain culture due to threatening acts by a few members of that culture. Negative stereotypes occur when the negative qualities of a few members of a cultural group are generalized to the entire group, or when actions of members of a certain cultural group are perceived negatively due to the cultural ignorance of outsiders.

**43. C:** This information supports the inference that health care and nutrition for children in Guatemala is poorer than it is in the United States and Singapore. This is a valid inference because the infant mortality rate in Guatemala is far higher than in the United States or Singapore, and because poor health care and nutrition are closely linked with high infant mortality. Although Guatemala's infant mortality rate is high, it is still lower than the world average of 42 deaths per 1,000 live births. This information does not indicate what the most common cause of death is for young children in Guatemala, and it does not indicate how many children are born in Guatemala overall.

**44. D:** Based on the information provided, it is most likely to be true that many Bangladeshis live in poverty. This inference is supported by the fact that individuals who are illiterate typically cannot secure middle-class jobs and instead toil in low-skill, low-wage jobs that do not pay enough to lift the worker out of poverty. Since nearly half of Bangladeshis are illiterate, it is highly unlikely that three-quarters of Bangladeshis work in the business and information sectors, because employment in these sectors requires basic literacy skills.

**45. D:** English, French, and Portuguese are all part of the Indo-European language family. French and Portuguese are part of the Romance subset of Indo-European languages, while English is part of the Germanic subset. Chinese is not part of the Indo-European language family, but instead is part of the Sino-Tibetan language family.

**46. B:** The majority of Russia's population is not Catholic. The largest religion in Russia is Orthodox Christianity, while at least 75 percent of the populations of Mexico, Spain, and Ireland identify themselves as Catholic. Catholicism spread from Rome throughout western Europe, although many northern European countries, like England, eventually converted to Protestantism. Ireland was an exception to this general rule. Since much of South and Central America was colonized by Spain, which has remained Catholic, most of these countries also have majority Catholic populations.

**47. D:** Laws that prevent women from owning property make it difficult for women to start businesses, and they also give men increased bargaining power in family relationships, since women cannot exert legal control over family finances. Legislative quotas and availability of microfinance actually give women increased political and economic power. Laws that outlaw divorce typically affect men and women equally, and their effect on women's economic status is minimal.

**48. C:** The growth of trade between India and Britain during the colonial era resulted in products from India, including tea, becoming staples of the British diet. Spices from India were also in great demand in Britain and other European countries. However, British citizens did not adopt other Indian cultural traits, such as religion and style of dress.

**49. A:** The introduction of television allowed citizens to see political events like speeches, revolutions, and wars play out firsthand. When citizens gained the ability to see politicians speak and observe firsthand the effects of overseas wars, this changed their perception of politicians and political events. For instance, politicians' physical appearance became increasingly important, since citizens throughout the country could now see live footage of candidates. Previously, very few citizens saw anything other than photos of the candidates.

**50. A:** Traditional eating patterns in the developing countries of Asia have eroded due mainly to the introduction of convenient and low-priced prepackaged and fast-food products. Just as traditional cooking methods and eating traditions have become less common in the United States since the introduction of fast, convenient alternatives to preparing meals, this same effect has occurred in developing Asian countries. The effect is especially pronounced in urban areas, where prepackaged food is more widely available, but it has taken hold to a limited extent in rural areas as well.

# Practice Test #2

**1. Which of the following ancient historical events occurred the latest in time?**

a. The last of the Punic Wars was ended
b. The Romans began world domination
c. The Mayans produced a new calendar
d. The Chinese first built their Great Wall

**2. Which of the following Roman authors lived the earliest in time?**

a. Ovid
b. Virgil
c. Cicero
d. Horace

**3. Which statement is true about Cleopatra?**

a. Cleopatra's union with Julius Caesar produced no offspring
b. Cleopatra and Mark Antony joined forces to oppose Caesar
c. Cleopatra committed suicide, and Mark Antony followed suit
d. Cleopatra was a member of the Greek royal Ptolemy family

**4. Which of the following was chronologically the latest action of Roman Emperor Constantine the Great?**

a. Issuing the Edict of Milan, legalizing Christianity
b. His conversion to the Christian religion himself
c. Establishing the new capital of Constantinople
d. Being the last to rule a unified Roman Empire

**5. Which tribal ruler deposed the last of the Roman emperors in Europe?**

a. Attila
b. Clovis
c. Odoacer
d. Theodoric

**6. During the early Medieval period in Europe, before the 5th century, where were the main centers of literacy found?**

a. They were in the homes of the wealthy
b. They were in the churches and monasteries
c. They were in the local artisan and craft guilds
d. There were no centers of literacy

**7. Which of the following is true of the feudal system of organization in Europe?**

a. It was first used in France by the Normans
b. It was first used in England by the Saxons
c. It was introduced to France by the English
d. It was a way to centralize the government

**8. Which of the following was a common factor related to the falls of both the Western Roman Empire in Europe and the Han Dynasty in China?**

a. Strict political ethics
b. Powerful conquerors
c. Government surpluses
d. Survival through religion

**9. Of the following, which civilization was NOT an influence on the development of the medieval Byzantine Empire?**

a. Greek civilization
b. Roman civilization
c. Eastern civilization
d. All of these

**10. Which statement is true about religious developments in medieval Byzantium?**

a. Islam overtook Christianity to develop a mainly Islamic civilization in Byzantium
b. Christianity overcame Islam to develop primarily Byzantine culture in Byzantium
c. Islam and Christianity respectively developed Islamic and Byzantine civilizations
d. Conflicts between Islam and Christianity prevented the growth of any civilization

**11. What is correct regarding conditions leading up to the Great Schism?**

a. There were no major differences within the Catholic Church in the 4th and 5th centuries
b. Differences between Eastern and Western Christianity built up for 700 years
c. Theological differences between East and West contributed but not language difference
d. The Great Schism was caused only by disagreements of the Eastern and Western bishops

**12. Which of these was a disagreement about Christian doctrine contributing to the Great Schism?**

a. The Eastern Orthodox Church rejected the idea of the Immaculate Conception
b. The Western Roman Catholic Church challenged the infallibility of Rome's Pope
c. The Eastern Orthodox Church was the only one embracing the idea of purgatory
d. The Roman Catholic Church rejected the insertion of "Son" to the Nicene Creed

**13. Which of the following events associated with the transition from the Middle Ages to the Renaissance in the Western world was the latest in time?**

a. Martin Luther's posting of his 95 Theses at Wittenberg
b. Christopher Columbus's ships landing in the Americas
c. The end to England and France's Hundred Years' War
d. Gutenberg inventing the movable-type printing press

**14. Which group led the Counterreformation in response to the Protestant Reformation?**

a. Anglicans
b. Lutherans
c. The Jesuits
d. Reformed

**15. Which two consecutive national dynasties were associated with a golden age in China when it led the world in wealth, power, and technology?**

a. The Han and Tang Dynasties
b. The Tang and Song Dynasties
c. The Han and Sui Dynasties
d. The Song and Sui Dynasties

**16. Which is true of innovations by China during its golden age from the 7th through the 13th centuries C.E.?**

a. Porcelain ceramics existed for years before this golden age
b. China imported mechanical clocks made in other countries
c. The production of paper money did not begin until later on
d. China developed magnetic compasses aiding sea navigation

**17. What is correct about cultural aspects of China's golden age from 689 to 1279 C.E.?**

a. The Song Dynasty was known for Li Bo's poetry
b. The Tang Dynasty was known for Tu Fu's poetry
c. The Tang Dynasty was known for Taoist painting
d. China had foreign trade but no foreign residents

**18. Who was best known as a poet of the early European Renaissance?**

a. Masaccio
b. Da Vinci
c. Petrarch
d. Donatello

**19. Prior to the Renaissance, who studied ancient Greek literature in Europe?**

a. Medieval Byzantine scholars
b. Medieval Islamic scholars
c. Medieval Latin scholars
d. No one

**20. In Western Europe, ancient Greek texts on which subjects were NOT studied in the Middle Ages but recovered in the Renaissance?**

a. Mathematics
b. Philosophy
c. Sciences
d. History

**21. Who is least associated with restoring the culture of classical Greek antiquity to Western Europe in the Renaissance, which prepared the way for the Protestant Reformation?**

a. Pico della Mirandola
b. Coluccio Salutati
c. Lorenzo Valla
d. Erasmus

**22. What is accurate regarding the beliefs of Martin Luther and other Protestant Reformers?**

a. They opposed many Catholic doctrines but not papal authority
b. They questioned Catholic beliefs about the roles of the saints
c. They had no issues around the doctrine of particular judgment
d. They at least agreed with Catholic attitudes on the Virgin Mary

**23. According to Martin Luther's own writing, which did he regard as the most central issue of the Protestant Reformation?**

a. The Catholic church's sale of indulgences
b. The Catholic church's belief in purgatory
c. The Catholic doctrine of freedom of will
d. The Catholic Pope's degree of authority

**24. Which of the following ancient civilizations of the Americas lived in Central America?**

a. The Incas
b. The Aztecs
c. All of these
d. The Mayans

**25. Of the following Pre-Columbian American civilizations, which one has descendants still living today?**

a. The Mayans
b. The Aztecs
c. The Incas
d. None

*Questions 26– 27 pertain to Figure 4:*

**Historical Population of Buffalo, New York**

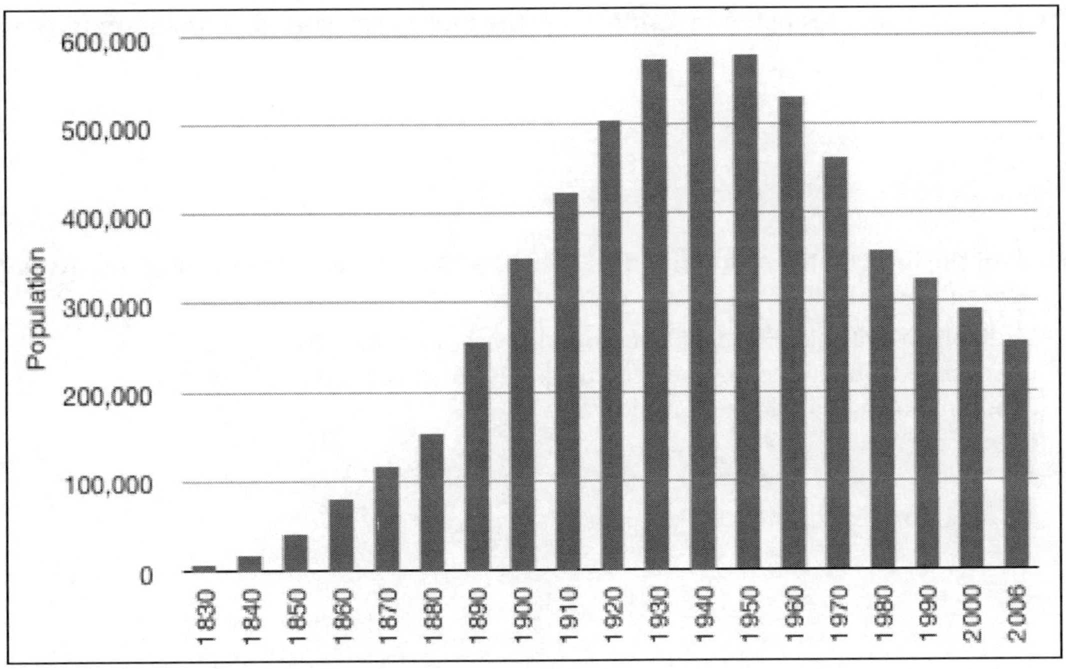

**26. The city of Buffalo, New York, used to be a major transit hub for commercial goods, but with the construction of the St. Lawrence Seaway, shipments could bypass Buffalo completely. This change dealt a major blow to the city's economy. Based on the information in Figure 4, one can infer that this change occurred during which decade?**

a. 1830s
b. 1910s
c. 1930s
d. 1950s

**27. Imagine that the creator of Figure 4 kept the physical size of the intervals on the vertical axis (y-axis) of the graph the same but labeled the intervals by 500,000 instead of 100,000. Which of the following statements best describes the effect that this would have on the graph?**

a. It would make the graph more precise and easy to read
b. It would mean that the intervals on the horizontal axis (x-axis) would have to be adjusted as well
c. It would mean that the changes in Buffalo's population would appear smaller than they do on the current graph
d. It wouldn't make any difference in the graph if the intervals were changed

*Questions 28 & 29 pertain to Table 3:*

**Population and Population Growth Rates for Four Countries**

| Country | Estimated Population (2011) | Estimated Annual Population Growth |
|---|---|---|
| **Russia** | 142,905,200 | –0.51% |
| **India** | 1,210,193,422 | 1.46% |
| **South Korea** | 48,988,833 | 0.33% |
| **Ethiopia** | 79,455,634 | 2.51% |

**28. Which of the countries listed in Table 3 has the lowest estimated annual population growth rate?**

a. Russia
b. India
c. South Korea
d. Ethiopia

**29. Based on the information provided in Table 3, which of the following statements is TRUE of South Korea's population?**

a. It is likely to overtake Ethiopia's population within the next five years
b. Its estimated annual population growth rate is about the same as Russia's
c. Its population is growing very rapidly
d. None of the above

**30. When political refugees choose a destination country, their HIGHEST priority is typically which of the following?**

a. Selecting a destination country that is accessible and likely to accept them as refugees
b. Moving to the most economically prosperous destination country available so that they can find jobs when they arrive
c. Selecting a destination country in which their relatives already live
d. Emigrating to a country in which their native language is spoken

**31. Which of the following is an example of an economic immigrant?**

a. A British businesswoman who visits India occasionally to oversee her company's operations there
b. A nurse from the Philippines who accepts a permanent job in the United States because it pays more than similar jobs in his home country
c. An American college student who accepts a temporary job as a nanny in Europe in order to experience a different culture
d. A woman who seeks asylum in the United States because her home country denies her basic rights due to her religion

**32. Which of the following phenomena had a positive influence on population growth in Europe?**

a. Immigration from Africa and the Middle East
b. Formation of the European Union
c. Restrictions on genetically modified foods
d. All of the above

**33. Increasing urbanization and population growth in cities typically result in which of the following?**

a. Lower prices for housing, food, and consumer goods in urban areas
b. Increased demand for resources and services in rural areas
c. Greater poverty and shorter life expectancy for all citizens
d. Increasing competition for low-wage jobs in urban areas

**34. In less developed countries, many citizens rely on a diet of fresh, seasonal foods purchased from local farmers. In the United States and other developed countries, citizens eat a diet consisting of both fresh and prepackaged foods that are often transported from distant farms in other states and even other countries. Which of the following statements provides the BEST explanation for these different diets?**

a. Food companies in developed countries have access to technological advances like food additives, refrigeration, and genetic modification that allow food to travel great distances while remaining fresh
b. In less developed countries, farmers do not have access to insecticides and modern farming equipment
c. People in less developed countries prefer to eat local food, and are not interested in purchasing prepackaged foods
d. People in developed countries are increasingly demanding that their food be organic and locally sourced

**35. Which of the following is NOT a common environmental effect of drought?**

a. Low crop yields
b. Desertification
c. Excessive irrigation
d. Wildfires

**36. Which of the following statements is TRUE of El Niño?**

a. It is caused by unusually cool surface temperatures in the Atlantic Gulf Stream
b. It produces extreme weather events like droughts and floods in certain parts of the world
c. It typically causes major crop failures in the United States and Europe
d. It occurs only about once every 100 years

**37. The growth of suburbs on the outskirts of metropolitan areas in the United States was facilitated by which of the following processes?**

a. The increasing availability of light rail, personal automobiles, and highways for commuting
b. The lack of infrastructure in urban centers
c. The abundance of services within walking distance of suburban housing
d. The lack of jobs in urban centers

**38. The Amazon, Congo, and Mississippi river basins are regions defined PRIMARILY by which of the following?**

a. Their climates
b. Their soil types
c. The amount of precipitation they receive
d. The outlet toward which their water drains

**39. Which of the following could MOST accurately be described as comprising a cultural region?**

a. All of the countries on the African continent
b. All of the Middle Eastern countries in which Arabic is spoken and Islam is practiced
c. All countries in the world that have democratic governments
d. All countries in Asia that have high levels of economic development

**40. Which of the following is an example of a functional cultural region?**

a. The southern United States
b. The State of California
c. The majority Catholic countries of southern Europe
d. The Spanish-speaking countries of Central America

**41. Perceptual cultural regions in the United States, such as the Creole cultural region in Louisiana and the Dixie cultural region in the southern United States, are strongly rooted in which of the following?**

a. Shared historical experiences and customs
b. Uniform levels of economic development
c. Distinctive ecosystems
d. Distinctive political systems

**42. Individuals who do not have direct experience with a given culture tend to think of that culture in which of the following ways?**

a. In terms of stereotypes that portray members of that culture negatively
b. In terms of simplified stereotypes that do not fully represent the diversity of the culture's individual members
c. In terms of assumptions about that culture that are based on fear of the unfamiliar
d. Both A and B

**43. In Country A, approximately 75 percent of citizens have access to the Internet. In Country B, only 15 percent of citizens have Internet access. Which of the following statements BEST describes the way in which lack of Internet access will affect citizens of Country B?**

a. Citizens of Country B will have lower literacy rates than citizens of Country A
b. Citizens of Country B will lack a valuable tool to exchange information and hold their government accountable
c. Citizens in Country B will not be able to maintain their traditional culture
d. Lack of Internet access will have little or no impact on the citizens of Country B

**44. Italy, Japan, and Greece have populations in which an unusually large proportion of their citizens are over the age of 65. This is likely to have which of the following effects on life in these countries?**

a. The quality of health care will decline
b. It will be more difficult for young people to find jobs
c. A larger portion of public and private resources will be necessary to care for the health and well-being of the aging population
d. The proportion of citizens who are of working and childbearing age will increase

**45. Written languages that are based on the Roman alphabet, such as English, are used in many countries throughout the world. On which of the following continents is use of the Roman alphabet LEAST common?**

a. Africa
b. Australia
c. South America
d. Asia

**46. Islam is NOT the primary religion in which of the following countries?**

a. Saudi Arabia
b. Indonesia
c. Egypt
d. Brazil

**47. In democratic countries, limited economic opportunities faced by members of religious minorities are typically a result of which of the following?**

a. Laws that bar members of certain religions from owning property
b. Discrimination against members of religious minorities in employment, education, and housing
c. Traditions that discourage educational attainment among members of religious minorities
d. Laws that restrict members of religious minorities from practicing their faith

**48. The wide availability of Italian, Mexican, and Chinese cuisines in the United States demonstrates which of the following processes?**

a. Immigration leading to economic growth
b. Immigration leading to cultural diffusion and change
c. Demand for cross-cultural experiences leading to immigration
d. Immigrants failing to assimilate

**49. Which of the following has NOT been a major effect of widespread Internet usage?**

a. Most citizens have become more knowledgeable about political and social issues
b. News can be disseminated to large audiences almost instantaneously
c. Citizens can more easily communicate with distant friends and family members
d. Citizens have convenient access to a broad range of information representing a wide spectrum of viewpoints

**50. Which of the following is an example of a grassroots cultural change that has occurred in the United States and other developed countries as a result of increasing concerns about environmental degradation?**

a. Implementation of federal emissions standards for vehicles
b. Implementation of laws requiring factories to install equipment that reduces air pollution
c. Creation of standards defining the legal limits for certain toxic substances in air and water
d. Increased voluntary participation in community recycling programs

# Answer Key and Explanations

**1. A:** The First Punic War began in 264 BC. In the Third, and last, Punic War, the Romans completely destroyed Carthage, ending all vestiges of the Carthaginian Empire in 146 BC. The Romans' world dominion had begun with their defeat of Seleucid King Antiochus III at the Battle of Thermopylae in 191 BC. The Mayans produced a new, more accurate calendar circa 300 BC. The Chinese first constructed the Great Wall of China circa 215 BC. Hence 146 BC, the end of the last Punic War, was the event latest in time.

**2. C:** Famous Roman orator, statesman, and political and philosophical writer Cicero, who introduced the Romans to Greek philosophy and humanism, lived from 106 to 43 BC. Roman poet Ovid, known for his Metamorphoses, lived from 43 BC to 14 AD. Roman poet Virgil, known for his Aeneid, lived from 70 to 19 BC. Horace, the Roman satirist and lyric poet, lived from 65 to 8 BC.

**3. D:** Cleopatra was a member of the Ptolemaic Dynasty, a Greek royal family who ruled Egypt during the Hellenistic Period after the death of Alexander the Great. Her union with Julius Caesar, which she arranged to reinforce her role as ruler, did produce a child, Caesarion, whom she later named as her co-ruler. His supporters named him Pharaoh briefly following Cleopatra's death, but he was then killed by Octavian (later called Caesar Augustus), Julius Caesar's heir and successor. Cleopatra joined with Mark Antony against Octavian, not against Julius Caesar, after Julius Caesar's assassination. Mark Antony committed suicide, and Cleopatra followed suit, not vice versa. (She had ordered her servants to tell him she was dead; believing this on top of being defeated by Octavian, Antony stabbed himself. Cleopatra saw him before he died; upon his death, she arranged her own suicide.)

**4. B:** Emperor Constantine the Great did much to further Christianity, such as issuing the Edict of Milan in 313 AD to legalize Christianity, but he only converted to the religion himself upon his deathbed in 337 AD. Constantine established a new Eastern capital of the Roman Empire in 330 AD in present-day Istanbul, named Constantinople after him at the time, upon the site of the former Byzantium. Constantine achieved a temporary reunification of the Eastern and Western parts of the Roman Empire. He was, however, not the last to rule a unified Roman Empire; Theodosius the Great was. By 395 AD, the Roman Empire had permanently divided into Eastern and Western Empires.

**5. C:** Odoacer's deposition of Romulus Augustulus, the last Roman Emperor, to become King of Italy in 476 is considered by historians as the ending of the Western Roman Empire. Attila the Hun and his "Mongol hordes" attacked Roman territories earlier in the 5th century. Clovis was a king of the Frankish tribe and ruled areas that are now France; he also converted to Christianity in 496, influencing public adoption of the religion. Theodoric the Great, an Ostrogoth (Eastern German tribal) king, was Odoacer's successor and established the Kingdom of Italy in place of Roman rule circa 496.

**6. B:** During the early Medieval period (or Middle Ages), Europe was characterized by widespread illiteracy, ignorance, and superstition once the unifying influence of the Roman Empire was lost. Few universities, like the university at Constantinople founded in 2 AD and those at Athens, Antioch, and Alexandria around the same time, existed then. Before the 5th and 6th centuries C.E., any education was conducted at cathedral or monastery schools or privately in the homes of wealthy families, which cannot be considered "main centers of literacy." More religious schools were created through Charlemagne's reforms in the 9th century, and early forms of universities began developing in the 11th and 12th centuries.

**7. A:** The Normans, a tribe associated with Normandy in France, began using the feudal system around 900 AD. It was not until the Norman invasion of England in 1066 by William the Conqueror, who deposed the last Saxon (a Germanic tribal ancestor of English, Dutch, and ethnic German peoples) king, that feudalism was introduced to England. Thereafter, it spread widely throughout Western Europe. Feudal systems typically developed where governments were not centralized as local alternatives. Feudalism only receded when strong, central monarchies were established in various European nations.

**8. D:** In China, religion helped people survive following the fall of the Han Dynasty; religion also helped Eastern Europeans to endure following the fall of the Western Roman Empire. Political corruption contributed to the falls of both empires rather than strict ethics. Neither of these empires fell to powerful conquerors but to multiple damages, including from corrupt politics; diseases; attacks by barbarian tribes; and government funding shortages, not surpluses, due to inadequate tax collections.

**9. D:** The medieval Byzantine Empire in Eastern Europe was influenced by all three civilizations: The Alexandrian/Hellenic civilization of the Greeks was native to the Mediterranean region; the Romans' subsequent conquest of the Greeks and other European civilizations contributed their widespread cultural influence; and influences from Eastern or Oriental civilizations were brought through trade, travel, and Byzantium's central location and major position as a world culture.

**10. C:** Medieval Byzantium incorporated influences from both Islam and Christianity. Due to inherent differences between the two religions, Islamic civilization was developed through Muslim influences, while Byzantine civilization was developed through Christian influences. Neither religion overtook the other to develop one primary culture in Byzantium. Due to its size, ethnic diversity, and multiple cultural influences, civilization grew in medieval Byzantium and was not prevented by conflicts between the religions.

**11. B:** Even when Christianity was first legalized in the Roman Empire by Constantine in 313 C.E., and even when it was the only religion recognized by Roman rule by the 5th century, major differences existed between the Eastern and Western Christian Churches. These built up over 700 years, leading to the 11th century's Great Schism in the Catholic Church of Europe. The differences were theological, political, social, cultural, and linguistic—the Eastern Church spoke Greek, while the Western Church spoke Latin. The Schism's causes were these multiple differences and not disagreements of bishops. In fact, one political difference was that the Western Church was led by one bishop in Rome, while the Eastern Church was governed by multiple bishops in different cities.

**12. A:** In addition to differences in language, culture, society, and politics, differences in theology contributed to the Great Schism dividing the Catholic Church into Roman Catholic and Eastern Orthodox Churches in the 11th century. Among these, the Eastern Orthodox Church rejected the doctrine of the Virgin Mary's Immaculate Conception of Jesus Christ, in which the Western Roman Catholic Church believed. The Roman Catholic Church also subscribed to the Roman Pope's infallibility regarding Church doctrine, but the Eastern Orthodox did not. Eastern Orthodox Christians also rejected the concept of purgatory, which was embraced by the Western Roman Catholics. Moreover, Roman Catholicism inserted ". . . and the Son" (after God) to the eighth article of the Nicene Creed, which established Christian doctrines, but the Eastern Orthodox objected to this addition as unauthorized.

**13. A:** Martin Luther posted his 95 Theses on the door of the cathedral at Wittenberg in 1517, outlining his reasons for breaking away from the Catholic Church. This reduced the power of Catholicism over Europe, allowing the intellectual inquiry and diversity of the Renaissance.

Columbus landed in the Americas in 1492, signaling the onset of European exploration and expansionism to other continents, which was compatible with Renaissance ideas. The Hundred Years' War between England and France ended in 1453. Thereafter England refocused its former continental domination to develop great naval forces, and European nations began creating more modern states and armies. Gutenberg's printing press invention in 1445 allowed mass publishing, enabling the public to become literate again after medieval illiteracy.

**14. C:** The Jesuits, a Catholic religious order, mounted the Counterreformation in reaction to the Protestant Reformation led by Martin Luther, John Calvin, and others. The Counterreformation restored Poland and other large parts of Europe to Catholicism. The Anglicans were one of the largest new Protestant denominations and were based in England. The Lutherans, named after Martin Luther, were another large, new Protestant denomination living in Germany and Scandinavia. The Reformed Churches were also one of the largest new Protestant denominations found in Scotland, the Netherlands, Switzerland, and Germany. The Protestant Reformation also included many other, smaller Protestant denominations.

**15. B:** The Tang and Song Dynasties were separated by 53 years, but during those interim years, only local dynasties ruled, and there was no national unity. Thus, the Tang and Song were consecutive national dynasties in China. These two dynastic periods created a golden age wherein China became the richest, most powerful, and most technologically advanced country in the world. The Han Dynasty fell in 220 C.E., while the Tang began in 618, so they were nowhere near consecutive. The Sui Dynasty followed the Han chronologically but did not begin until 581—361 years after the Han fell—and the Sui, while responsible for major public accomplishments, only lasted 37 years before being overthrown by peasants. The Song Dynasty ruled from 960 to 1279, while the Sui ruled much earlier, from 581 to 618—not consecutive in either order.

**16. D:** The Chinese did develop the magnetic compass during its golden age under the Tang and Song Dynasties, which improved nautical navigation, allowing more sea trade. During this golden age, the Chinese developed porcelain (a very fine ceramic made from kaolin, a very pure clay), which did not exist previously. The Chinese also developed mechanical clocks, rather than importing them from other countries, during this period of growth. This time period also did include the Chinese innovation of producing paper money.

**17. B:** Tu Fu was a great poet during the Tang Dynasty's reign in China. Li Bo was another great poet, also during the Tang Dynasty and not the Song. Exquisite paintings showing Taoist influences were created in China during the later Song Dynasty rather than the earlier Tang period. During the golden age encompassing both the Tang and Song Dynasties' reigns, China not only engaged in much foreign trade, but it also hosted many foreign residents as Arab and other traders came there for commerce and stayed to live in China's flourishing cities.

**18. C:** Petrarch was an Italian best known for his lyrical poetry, particularly sonnets, as well as being a scholar. He was also one of the first humanists and originated the idea of the "Dark Ages" to describe the Middle Ages before the Renaissance. Masaccio and Donatello were both famous as Italian Renaissance painters. Leonardo Da Vinci was a polymath with many talents, but he was known more for his drawings, paintings, sculptures, architecture, scientific inventions, and so on. He was also a mathematician, engineer, botanist, geologist, anatomist, cartographer, and writer but was not known as a poet.

**19. A:** In the Middle Ages, only Byzantine scholars studied literary works by the ancient Greeks. Medieval Islamic and Latin scholars studied ancient Greek texts but only those devoted to mathematics, sciences, philosophy, and theology. Greek works of drama, poetry, oratory, and history were only studied by medieval Byzantine scholars. It was not until the Renaissance that Latin and Islamic scholars in Western Europe regained access to the literary works of ancient Greece, creating a Greek revival and contributing to Renaissance Humanism.

**20. D:** History was one subject within ancient Greek texts that Western Europe's Latin and Islamic scholars did not study during the Middle Ages, when most of the knowledge and culture of ancient Greece and Rome was lost there. Poetry and dramatic and oratorical works were also not studied by Western European scholars in the Middle Ages. In medieval times, these scholars only studied ancient Greek texts covering mathematics, the sciences, philosophy, and theology. Only the Byzantine scholars of Eastern Europe studied ancient Greek literary and historical texts during the Middle Ages. Western European scholars in the Renaissance first recovered ancient Latin works, and then ancient Greek works, and studied them, informing the Renaissance Humanist movement.

**21. A:** Giovanni Pico della Mirandola's On the Dignity of Man was considered the "Renaissance Manifesto" and a vital contribution to Renaissance Humanism. However, della Mirandola's thinking was eventually influenced by anti-Humanist Savonarola. While well educated in Greek, Aramaic, and Hebrew, as well as Latin, as he believed any good Biblical scholar should be, della Mirandola was not as closely associated with the revival of ancient Greek culture that prepared Europe for the Protestant Reformation as the others: Renaissance scholar Coluccio Salutati invited Manuel Chrysoloras, a Byzantine scholar and diplomat, to come teach Greek in Florence, Italy, prompting a movement to reintegrate ancient Greek literary and historical works into Western European curricula. Lorenzo Valla and Erasmus were both Catholic priests and Renaissance Humanists. Italian educator Valla improved Latin style, restoring it to more classical forms and was admired by Martin Luther who started the Protestant Reformation. Erasmus a Dutch scholar prepared new Greek and Latin versions of the New Testament informed by the original Greek New Testament, raising issues influencing the Protestant Reformation.

**22. B:** Among a great many differences of opinion the Protestant Reformers found against the Catholic Church, one was its beliefs about the intercession of the saints and its devotion to them, which Luther criticized in his 95 Theses as excessive. They opposed many Catholic doctrines, including the Pope's authority, which Luther's Theses also decried. The first Protestants did disagree with the Catholic doctrine of particular judgment (the judgment of an individual person upon dying, as distinguished from the belief in the general Last Judgment of everybody when the world's end). Moreover, they disagreed with Catholic attitudes toward Mary, including their belief in Immaculate (virgin) Conception of Jesus and the extent of Catholic devotion to Mary.

**23. C:** While various issues Martin Luther raised in his 95 Theses have often been cited as central, including the Catholic selling of indulgences, belief in purgatory, belief in the Pope's infallibility, and the issue of the Pope's political authority, Luther himself wrote that these were trivial compared to the truly central issue: the Catholic doctrine of free will. In 1524, Desiderius Erasmus had published De Libero Arbitrio (On Free Will), attacking Luther's beliefs. In 1525, Luther replied, refuting Erasmus in his De Servo Arbitrio (On the Bondage of the Will, or literally, On the Unfree Will). He wrote that "the papacy, purgatory, indulgences and such like . . ." were "trifles, rather than issues . . ." and thanked Erasmus for attacking "the real thing, that is, the essential issue," that is, free will. Luther believed that, after Adam's fall, free will was no longer truly free.

**24. D:** The ancient Mayan civilization was located in Central America. Today, the land of their former empire comprises Guatemala, Belize, Honduras, and El Salvador in Central America and also the Yucatan peninsula and the south of Mexico. The ancient civilization of the Incas was located in what is now Peru in South America. The ancient civilization of the Aztecs lived in what is Mexico today.

**25. A:** There are many descendants of the ancient Mayans still living today in southern Mexico, Central America, and on the Yucatan peninsula. However, the Aztec and Inca civilizations were destroyed in the 16th century by the Spanish conquistadores, who first exposed them to foreign diseases like smallpox, decimating the natives' numbers, and then attacked and killed the remaining populations. The Mayans' decentralization allowed them to resist these invaders for 170 years, and moreover, many independent states enabled their peoples to survive even after Spanish political conquest.

**26. D:** One can infer that the St. Lawrence Seaway was most likely built during the 1950s, because this is when the city's population first began to decline. A decline in a major industry (in this case the transport of commercial goods) typically causes a decline in population, since residents seek jobs elsewhere.

**27. C:** If the intervals were relabeled by 500,000 instead of 100,000, it would mean that the changes in Buffalo's population would seem smaller than they do on the current graph. This is because Buffalo's population has never been more than 600,000, so the upper portion of the chart at intervals of 1 million, 1.5 million, and higher would be completely unused. None of the bars would reach higher than the second interval on the graph's y-axis.

**28. A:** Russia has the lowest estimated annual population growth rate at –0.51 percent. This means that Russia's population is actually declining, rather than growing. South Korea has the second lowest rate at 0.33 percent.

**29. D:** South Korea's population will not overtake Ethiopia's because Ethiopia's population is growing much faster than South Korea's. South Korea's population growth rate is not similar to Russia's because Russia's population is declining, while South Korea's is growing. It is also not true that South Korea's population is growing very rapidly. Its growth rate of 0.33 percent is moderate compared with India's and Ethiopia's.

**30. A:** When political refugees choose a destination country, their highest priority is typically selecting a destination country that is accessible and likely to accept them as refugees. If the country that they petition for refugee status does not accept them, they could be returned to their home country and subjected to further danger. The economy and culture of the destination country are generally secondary to concerns about safety.

**31. B:** A nurse from the Philippines who takes a permanent job in the United States because it pays more than similar jobs in his home country is an economic migrant. In this case, his main reason for immigrating to the United States is to pursue an economic opportunity that is not available in his home country. A student who travels abroad to gain cross-cultural experience may be earning money, but her primary objective is not to pursue economic opportunity.

**32. A:** Neither the formation of the European Union nor restrictions on genetically modified foods has contributed noticeably to Europe's population growth. However, immigration from Africa and the Middle East has increased the overall population and the population growth rate.

**33. D:** Increasing urbanization and population growth in cities typically result in increasing competition for low-wage jobs in urban areas. As the population of a city swells, prices for housing, food, and consumer goods typically increase, since the supply cannot keep up with demand. The need for resources and services in rural areas is likely to decline or remain steady, since urbanization typically entails migration from rural areas to urban areas. Migrants from rural areas are often less educated individuals in search of an alternative to agriculture, so competition for low-skill, low-wage jobs increases in cities. An influx of more highly educated migrants can also have this effect, as educated jobseekers who cannot secure white collar jobs join the pool of workers in search of blue collar ones.

**34. A:** Food companies in developed countries have access to technological advances like food additives, refrigeration, and genetic modification that allow food to travel great distances while remaining fresh, which allows the companies to provide a variety of fresh foods year around, as well as a large assortment of packaged foods that keep for long periods of time. Since these advances are less widely available in less developed countries, citizens there tend to rely on a more traditional diet of locally sourced foods.

**35. C:** Excessive irrigation is not a common environmental effect of drought, but rather a factor that exacerbates the severity of droughts. Wildfires, poor crop yields, and desertification are all common results of drought conditions. All of these phenomena can have devastating effects on humans because they can destroy food supplies and reduce the amount of arable land that is available even after the drought has passed.

**36. B:** El Niño is known for producing extreme weather events like droughts and floods in certain parts of the world. It is caused by variations in the ocean surface temperature and air pressure in the western Pacific, not the Atlantic Ocean. Its effects can be felt as far away as Africa, Australia, and Asia, where droughts and tropical cyclones often result.

**37. A:** The growth of suburbs on the outskirts of metropolitan areas in the United States was facilitated by the increasing availability of light rail, personal automobiles, and highways for commuting. In large metropolitan areas like New York City, suburbanization has been facilitated primarily by the introduction of light rail systems. However, the process is much more commonly facilitated through the introduction of improved roadways and a level of economic development that places car ownership within reach of the average middle-class worker.

**38. D:** The Amazon, Congo, and Mississippi river basins are regions defined primarily by the outlet toward which their water flows. The main criterion for an area's inclusion in one of these regions is that its water drains toward the main river (the Amazon, Congo, and Mississippi), and then onward to that river's main outlet. These are the three largest river basins in the world.

**39. B:** All of the Middle Eastern countries in which Arabic is spoken and Islam is practiced could be accurately described as comprising a cultural region. A cultural region is any area in which inhabitants generally share one or more cultural characteristics, such as language or religion. Form of government and level of economic development are not cultural characteristics, although they are sometimes linked to certain cultural practices. Inhabitants of African countries do not share any unifying cultural trait, since the continent is characterized by a wide variety of languages, religions, colonial influences, and social customs.

**40. B:** The State of California is a functional cultural region because it has a central organizational node (the seat of government in the state capital) and it is organized to function economically and politically as a single unit. The majority Catholic southern European countries, as well as the Spanish-speaking countries of Central America, constitute formal cultural regions, because their inhabitants share certain cultural traits. However, they lack central organizational structures that would define them as functional cultural regions. The Southern United States is often considered to be a perceptual cultural region, but it also lacks a central organizational structure and clearly defined boundaries.

**41. A:** Perceptual cultural regions in the United States, such as the Creole culture region in Louisiana, and the Dixie cultural region in the southern United States, are strongly rooted in shared historical experiences and customs. This perception of a shared history helps define the members of and boundaries of these cultural regions. They are not defined by uniform levels of economic development, nor are they characterized by ecosystems or political systems that distinguish them from the rest of the United States.

**42. B:** Individuals who do not have direct experience with a given culture tend to think of that culture in terms of simplified stereotypes that do not fully represent the diversity of the culture's individual members. Many cultures have positive stereotypes associated with them, as well as negative ones. Positive cultural stereotypes can still be harmful to members of the culture who do not meet the expectations expressed in those stereotypes. Just as cultural stereotypes are not always negative, they are also based on a variety of assumptions about the target culture, and they may or may not be a response to an assumption that members of the target culture are threatening.

**43. B:** The main way that lack of Internet access will affect citizens of Country B is that they will not have access to a valuable tool to exchange information and hold their government accountable. While high levels of Internet access are correlated with high literacy rates, Internet access is not a cause of higher literacy rates. In fact, high literacy rates make use of and demand for Internet access possible. Use of the Internet tends to draw citizens, especially young people, away from traditional cultural practices as they gain exposure to global culture.

**44. C:** A larger portion of public and private resources will be necessary to care for the health and well-being of the aging population. The larger share of the population that is past retirement age should actually have a positive effect on the availability of jobs. It will increase expenditures on healthcare overall, but it should not affect the overall quality of care one way or another. As the proportion of citizens over 65 increases, the percentage of the population that is of working and childbearing age will decrease.

**45. D:** Use of the Roman alphabet is least common in Asia, because written languages like Chinese, Japanese, Korean, and Hindi were developed independently of the historical influences that shaped the languages of European countries and their colonies. Most areas in Africa, South America, and Australia that were colonized by European countries adopted the Roman alphabet.

**46. D:** Islam is not the primary religion in Brazil. It is the dominant religion in Indonesia, Saudi Arabia, and Egypt, as well as many other countries throughout Asia and Northern Africa.

**47. B:** In democratic countries, the limited economic opportunities faced by members of religious minorities are typically a result of discrimination in employment, education, and housing. Democratic constitutions typically prohibit laws that explicitly discriminate against religious minorities, and often they prohibit discrimination outright. However, economic discrimination can be subtle and difficult to eradicate.

**48. B:** The wide availability of Italian, Mexican, and Chinese cuisines in the United States demonstrates the process of immigration leading to cultural diffusion and change. As Chinese, Italian, and Mexican immigrants have arrived in the United States, they have introduced their native cuisines, which have become staples of the American diet. Although this cultural change came to pass when entrepreneurial immigrants opened restaurants to share their native cuisines, the popularity of these cuisines in and of itself is not an example of economic growth.

**49. A:** It is not true that widespread Internet usage has made citizens more knowledgeable about political and social issues. While the Internet does offer a wide variety of information representing a broad spectrum of viewpoints, this information is not necessarily well organized or high quality.

Furthermore, political scientists have not found any relationship between Internet usage and degree of knowledge about social issues.

**50. A:** Increased voluntary participation in community recycling programs is an example of a grassroots cultural change that has occurred in the United States and other developed countries as a result of increasing concerns about environmental degradation. The other examples provided are changes initiated by the government, so they are not examples of grassroots cultural change.

# How to Overcome Test Anxiety

Just the thought of taking a test is enough to make most people a little nervous. A test is an important event that can have a long-term impact on your future, so it's important to take it seriously and it's natural to feel anxious about performing well. But just because anxiety is normal, that doesn't mean that it's helpful in test taking, or that you should simply accept it as part of your life. Anxiety can have a variety of effects. These effects can be mild, like making you feel slightly nervous, or severe, like blocking your ability to focus or remember even a simple detail.

If you experience test anxiety—whether severe or mild—it's important to know how to beat it. To discover this, first you need to understand what causes test anxiety.

## Causes of Test Anxiety

While we often think of anxiety as an uncontrollable emotional state, it can actually be caused by simple, practical things. One of the most common causes of test anxiety is that a person does not feel adequately prepared for their test. This feeling can be the result of many different issues such as poor study habits or lack of organization, but the most common culprit is time management. Starting to study too late, failing to organize your study time to cover all of the material, or being distracted while you study will mean that you're not well prepared for the test. This may lead to cramming the night before, which will cause you to be physically and mentally exhausted for the test. Poor time management also contributes to feelings of stress, fear, and hopelessness as you realize you are not well prepared but don't know what to do about it.

Other times, test anxiety is not related to your preparation for the test but comes from unresolved fear. This may be a past failure on a test, or poor performance on tests in general. It may come from comparing yourself to others who seem to be performing better or from the stress of living up to expectations. Anxiety may be driven by fears of the future—how failure on this test would affect your educational and career goals. These fears are often completely irrational, but they can still negatively impact your test performance.

## Elements of Test Anxiety

As mentioned earlier, test anxiety is considered to be an emotional state, but it has physical and mental components as well. Sometimes you may not even realize that you are suffering from test anxiety until you notice the physical symptoms. These can include trembling hands, rapid heartbeat, sweating, nausea, and tense muscles. Extreme anxiety may lead to fainting or vomiting. Obviously, any of these symptoms can have a negative impact on testing. It is important to recognize them as soon as they begin to occur so that you can address the problem before it damages your performance.

The mental components of test anxiety include trouble focusing and inability to remember learned information. During a test, your mind is on high alert, which can help you recall information and stay focused for an extended period of time. However, anxiety interferes with your mind's natural processes, causing you to blank out, even on the questions you know well. The strain of testing during anxiety makes it difficult to stay focused, especially on a test that may take several hours. Extreme anxiety can take a huge mental toll, making it difficult not only to recall test information but even to understand the test questions or pull your thoughts together.

## Effects of Test Anxiety

Test anxiety is like a disease—if left untreated, it will get progressively worse. Anxiety leads to poor performance, and this reinforces the feelings of fear and failure, which in turn lead to poor performances on subsequent tests. It can grow from a mild nervousness to a crippling condition. If allowed to progress, test anxiety can have a big impact on your schooling, and consequently on your future.

Test anxiety can spread to other parts of your life. Anxiety on tests can become anxiety in any stressful situation, and blanking on a test can turn into panicking in a job situation. But fortunately, you don't have to let anxiety rule your testing and determine your grades. There are a number of relatively simple steps you can take to move past anxiety and function normally on a test and in the rest of life.

## Physical Steps for Beating Test Anxiety

While test anxiety is a serious problem, the good news is that it can be overcome. It doesn't have to control your ability to think and remember information. While it may take time, you can begin taking steps today to beat anxiety.

Just as your first hint that you may be struggling with anxiety comes from the physical symptoms, the first step to treating it is also physical. Rest is crucial for having a clear, strong mind. If you are tired, it is much easier to give in to anxiety. But if you establish good sleep habits, your body and mind will be ready to perform optimally, without the strain of exhaustion. Additionally, sleeping well helps you to retain information better, so you're more likely to recall the answers when you see the test questions.

Getting good sleep means more than going to bed on time. It's important to allow your brain time to relax. Take study breaks from time to time so it doesn't get overworked, and don't study right before bed. Take time to rest your mind before trying to rest your body, or you may find it difficult to fall asleep.

Along with sleep, other aspects of physical health are important in preparing for a test. Good nutrition is vital for good brain function. Sugary foods and drinks may give a burst of energy but this burst is followed by a crash, both physically and emotionally. Instead, fuel your body with protein and vitamin-rich foods.

Also, drink plenty of water. Dehydration can lead to headaches and exhaustion, especially if your brain is already under stress from the rigors of the test. Particularly if your test is a long one, drink water during the breaks. And if possible, take an energy-boosting snack to eat between sections.

Along with sleep and diet, a third important part of physical health is exercise. Maintaining a steady workout schedule is helpful, but even taking 5-minute study breaks to walk can help get your blood pumping faster and clear your head. Exercise also releases endorphins, which contribute to a positive feeling and can help combat test anxiety.

When you nurture your physical health, you are also contributing to your mental health. If your body is healthy, your mind is much more likely to be healthy as well. So take time to rest, nourish your body with healthy food and water, and get moving as much as possible. Taking these physical steps will make you stronger and more able to take the mental steps necessary to overcome test anxiety.

## Mental Steps for Beating Test Anxiety

Working on the mental side of test anxiety can be more challenging, but as with the physical side, there are clear steps you can take to overcome it. As mentioned earlier, test anxiety often stems from lack of preparation, so the obvious solution is to prepare for the test. Effective studying may be the most important weapon you have for beating test anxiety, but you can and should employ several other mental tools to combat fear.

First, boost your confidence by reminding yourself of past success—tests or projects that you aced. If you're putting as much effort into preparing for this test as you did for those, there's no reason you should expect to fail here. Work hard to prepare; then trust your preparation.

Second, surround yourself with encouraging people. It can be helpful to find a study group, but be sure that the people you're around will encourage a positive attitude. If you spend time with others who are anxious or cynical, this will only contribute to your own anxiety. Look for others who are motivated to study hard from a desire to succeed, not from a fear of failure.

Third, reward yourself. A test is physically and mentally tiring, even without anxiety, and it can be helpful to have something to look forward to. Plan an activity following the test, regardless of the outcome, such as going to a movie or getting ice cream.

When you are taking the test, if you find yourself beginning to feel anxious, remind yourself that you know the material. Visualize successfully completing the test. Then take a few deep, relaxing breaths and return to it. Work through the questions carefully but with confidence, knowing that you are capable of succeeding.

Developing a healthy mental approach to test taking will also aid in other areas of life. Test anxiety affects more than just the actual test—it can be damaging to your mental health and even contribute to depression. It's important to beat test anxiety before it becomes a problem for more than testing.

## Study Strategy

Being prepared for the test is necessary to combat anxiety, but what does being prepared look like? You may study for hours on end and still not feel prepared. What you need is a strategy for test prep. The next few pages outline our recommended steps to help you plan out and conquer the challenge of preparation.

### Step 1: Scope Out the Test

Learn everything you can about the format (multiple choice, essay, etc.) and what will be on the test. Gather any study materials, course outlines, or sample exams that may be available. Not only will this help you to prepare, but knowing what to expect can help to alleviate test anxiety.

### Step 2: Map Out the Material

Look through the textbook or study guide and make note of how many chapters or sections it has. Then divide these over the time you have. For example, if a book has 15 chapters and you have five days to study, you need to cover three chapters each day. Even better, if you have the time, leave an extra day at the end for overall review after you have gone through the material in depth.

If time is limited, you may need to prioritize the material. Look through it and make note of which sections you think you already have a good grasp on, and which need review. While you are studying, skim quickly through the familiar sections and take more time on the challenging parts.

Write out your plan so you don't get lost as you go. Having a written plan also helps you feel more in control of the study, so anxiety is less likely to arise from feeling overwhelmed at the amount to cover.

### Step 3: Gather Your Tools

Decide what study method works best for you. Do you prefer to highlight in the book as you study and then go back over the highlighted portions? Or do you type out notes of the important information? Or is it helpful to make flashcards that you can carry with you? Assemble the pens, index cards, highlighters, post-it notes, and any other materials you may need so you won't be distracted by getting up to find things while you study.

If you're having a hard time retaining the information or organizing your notes, experiment with different methods. For example, try color-coding by subject with colored pens, highlighters, or post-it notes. If you learn better by hearing, try recording yourself reading your notes so you can listen while in the car, working out, or simply sitting at your desk. Ask a friend to quiz you from your flashcards, or try teaching someone the material to solidify it in your mind.

### Step 4: Create Your Environment

It's important to avoid distractions while you study. This includes both the obvious distractions like visitors and the subtle distractions like an uncomfortable chair (or a too-comfortable couch that makes you want to fall asleep). Set up the best study environment possible: good lighting and a comfortable work area. If background music helps you focus, you may want to turn it on, but otherwise keep the room quiet. If you are using a computer to take notes, be sure you don't have any other windows open, especially applications like social media, games, or anything else that could distract you. Silence your phone and turn off notifications. Be sure to keep water close by so you stay hydrated while you study (but avoid unhealthy drinks and snacks).

Also, take into account the best time of day to study. Are you freshest first thing in the morning? Try to set aside some time then to work through the material. Is your mind clearer in the afternoon or evening? Schedule your study session then. Another method is to study at the same time of day that you will take the test, so that your brain gets used to working on the material at that time and will be ready to focus at test time.

### Step 5: Study!

Once you have done all the study preparation, it's time to settle into the actual studying. Sit down, take a few moments to settle your mind so you can focus, and begin to follow your study plan. Don't give in to distractions or let yourself procrastinate. This is your time to prepare so you'll be ready to fearlessly approach the test. Make the most of the time and stay focused.

Of course, you don't want to burn out. If you study too long you may find that you're not retaining the information very well. Take regular study breaks. For example, taking five minutes out of every hour to walk briskly, breathing deeply and swinging your arms, can help your mind stay fresh.

As you get to the end of each chapter or section, it's a good idea to do a quick review. Remind yourself of what you learned and work on any difficult parts. When you feel that you've mastered the material, move on to the next part. At the end of your study session, briefly skim through your notes again.

But while review is helpful, cramming last minute is NOT. If at all possible, work ahead so that you won't need to fit all your study into the last day. Cramming overloads your brain with more information than it can process and retain, and your tired mind may struggle to recall even previously learned information when it is overwhelmed with last-minute study. Also, the urgent nature of cramming and the stress placed on your brain contribute to anxiety. You'll be more likely to go to the test feeling unprepared and having trouble thinking clearly.

So don't cram, and don't stay up late before the test, even just to review your notes at a leisurely pace. Your brain needs rest more than it needs to go over the information again. In fact, plan to finish your studies by noon or early afternoon the day before the test. Give your brain the rest of the day to relax or focus on other things, and get a good night's sleep. Then you will be fresh for the test and better able to recall what you've studied.

### Step 6: Take a Practice Test

Many courses offer sample tests, either online or in the study materials. This is an excellent resource to check whether you have mastered the material, as well as to prepare for the test format and environment.

Check the test format ahead of time: the number of questions, the type (multiple choice, free response, etc.), and the time limit. Then create a plan for working through them. For example, if you have 30 minutes to take a 60-question test, your limit is 30 seconds per question. Spend less time on the questions you know well so that you can take more time on the difficult ones.

If you have time to take several practice tests, take the first one open book, with no time limit. Work through the questions at your own pace and make sure you fully understand them. Gradually work up to taking a test under test conditions: sit at a desk with all study materials put away and set a timer. Pace yourself to make sure you finish the test with time to spare and go back to check your answers if you have time.

After each test, check your answers. On the questions you missed, be sure you understand why you missed them. Did you misread the question (tests can use tricky wording)? Did you forget the information? Or was it something you hadn't learned? Go back and study any shaky areas that the practice tests reveal.

Taking these tests not only helps with your grade, but also aids in combating test anxiety. If you're already used to the test conditions, you're less likely to worry about it, and working through tests until you're scoring well gives you a confidence boost. Go through the practice tests until you feel comfortable, and then you can go into the test knowing that you're ready for it.

## Test Tips

On test day, you should be confident, knowing that you've prepared well and are ready to answer the questions. But aside from preparation, there are several test day strategies you can employ to maximize your performance.

First, as stated before, get a good night's sleep the night before the test (and for several nights before that, if possible). Go into the test with a fresh, alert mind rather than staying up late to study.

Try not to change too much about your normal routine on the day of the test. It's important to eat a nutritious breakfast, but if you normally don't eat breakfast at all, consider eating just a protein bar. If you're a coffee drinker, go ahead and have your normal coffee. Just make sure you time it so that the caffeine doesn't wear off right in the middle of your test. Avoid sugary beverages, and drink enough water to stay hydrated but not so much that you need a restroom break 10 minutes into the test. If your test isn't first thing in the morning, consider going for a walk or doing a light workout before the test to get your blood flowing.

Allow yourself enough time to get ready, and leave for the test with plenty of time to spare so you won't have the anxiety of scrambling to arrive in time. Another reason to be early is to select a good seat. It's helpful to sit away from doors and windows, which can be distracting. Find a good seat, get out your supplies, and settle your mind before the test begins.

When the test begins, start by going over the instructions carefully, even if you already know what to expect. Make sure you avoid any careless mistakes by following the directions.

Then begin working through the questions, pacing yourself as you've practiced. If you're not sure on an answer, don't spend too much time on it, and don't let it shake your confidence. Either skip it and come back later, or eliminate as many wrong answers as possible and guess among the remaining ones. Don't dwell on these questions as you continue—put them out of your mind and focus on what lies ahead.

Be sure to read all of the answer choices, even if you're sure the first one is the right answer. Sometimes you'll find a better one if you keep reading. But don't second-guess yourself if you do immediately know the answer. Your gut instinct is usually right. Don't let test anxiety rob you of the information you know.

If you have time at the end of the test (and if the test format allows), go back and review your answers. Be cautious about changing any, since your first instinct tends to be correct, but make sure you didn't misread any of the questions or accidentally mark the wrong answer choice. Look over any you skipped and make an educated guess.

At the end, leave the test feeling confident. You've done your best, so don't waste time worrying about your performance or wishing you could change anything. Instead, celebrate the successful completion of this test. And finally, use this test to learn how to deal with anxiety even better next time.

**Review Video: Test Anxiety**
Visit mometrix.com/academy and enter code: 100340

## Important Qualification

Not all anxiety is created equal. If your test anxiety is causing major issues in your life beyond the classroom or testing center, or if you are experiencing troubling physical symptoms related to your anxiety, it may be a sign of a serious physiological or psychological condition. If this sounds like your situation, we strongly encourage you to seek professional help.

# Additional Bonus Material

Due to our efforts to try to keep this book to a manageable length, we've created a link that will give you access to all of your additional bonus material:

**mometrix.com/bonus948/regglhistgeo**